Raising Spiritual Children in a Material World

PHIL CATALFO

BERKLEY BOOKS, NEW YORK

RAISING SPIRITUAL CHILDREN IN A MATERIAL WORLD

A Berkley Book / published by arrangement with
the author

PRINTING HISTORY
Berkley trade paperback edition / April 1997

The Putnam Berkley World Wide Web site address is
http://www.berkley.com/berkley

ISBN: 0-425-14954-4

Dedication

To my family:

MICHELLE—life partner, soul mate, my starting point and destination;

JESSAMINE—beauteous flower, light of my life, joyous being, noted scholar-aesthete, chillin'est kid there is;

PETER—rock of ages, inexhaustible energy source, distinguished artist, world-class athlete, budding herpetologist; and

GABRIEL—messenger of God, All-Star's All-Star, lionheart, resident Buddha (Hulk Hogan division), bravest boy—no, bravest *person*—I know.

Acknowledgments

The seed for this book was first planted in my brain by Peggy Taylor (although she would hasten to point out that she merely intended for me to write an *article*, for cryin' out loud). It was only about the ten-millionth time she had put her finger on something urgently interesting in the lives of her readers and peers. Whether I have served that interest or attained the altitude of her vision I cannot say, but one thing I *can* say is that this project has been a profound gift in my life, and if I didn't already have countless reasons to be eternally grateful to her, this would be all the reason I needed. Thanks, Peggy, and I promise never to run this long again.

Acknowledgments

While I was working on the book-disguised-as-an-article for Peggy and *New Age Journal,* I got a call from Stephanie Hamilton at *Parenting* magazine, asking if I'd be interested in doing a piece on talking to kids about God. This assignment convinced me to devote myself to a longer treatment of spirituality among contemporary families. For recommending me for the assignment, I thank Cynthia Rubin, my first editor and friend at *Parenting;* for letting me follow my unorthodox impulses and confirming me on the path to this book, I thank Stephanie. I hope they were as pleased with the resulting article, and this ensuing book, as I was to have had the opportunity.

After I finished work on the articles and started thinking seriously about doing a book, I met with Jack Mingo and Mark Friedman, who were the first to express interest in publishing it. They suggested a title that I began using as a subtitle, but which provoked much more interest among publishers and editors than my preferred title. Their suggestion ultimately evolved into the title of this book, so I thank them for the gift of a few words that conveyed what I was driving at more clearly than I could have on my own.

I always tuned out writers' acknowledgments right about the time they started thanking their agents. That was before I needed one, and found the ultimate package: Laurie Fox, a fiercely loyal and effective pro

Acknowledgments

who also was a thoroughly wonderful person and became a dear friend. (Honestly, Laurie, you didn't *have*
to move 500 miles just to be within four blocks of me,
but I will always cherish that dedication.) For going
to bat for me every time I couldn't get up the nerve
to face a publishing-biz curveball at the knees, I nom-
inate Laurie as my own personal Manny Mota. For
welcoming me to the fold years before I had a project
worthy of their time, for gently nagging me to offer
this book to the world, for finding it a good home
and the kind of conditions every writer deserves but
few writers get, and especially, for making it possible
for me to fulfill a lifelong dream, I thank Laurie and
her ab-fab boss, Linda Chester, who treated me as a
professional while I was still struggling with the concept.

In our first conversation, my editor, Hillary Cige,
displayed an enthusiasm for my idea I never hoped
to find in anyone outside my own head, let alone in
someone who would be in a position to judge my
work. Her faith in me and my vision, and her patience
during a most difficult time in my family's life—which
meant several delays in the completion of this book—
inspired me to undertake this project, and made it
possible for me to finish it under something like hu-
mane circumstances.

My dearest friend, Alan Reder, himself an accomplished author, cajoled and scolded and fretted over me, as he has for nearly thirty years, being the more together of the two of us. I hope he knows I took his every word to heart; I hope this book convinces him his effort didn't go for naught; I hope I can continue to count on his fierce counsel and blessed friendship for another 300 years, at least.

Many other writers, editors, and friends also offered specific advice and general encouragement in long measure: Howard Rheingold, Thaisa Frank, Mary Mackey, Joe Flower, Jon Carroll, Alice Kahn, and the legion denizens of the Writers conference on The WELL; Gerald Rosen, Wes Nisker, Barbara Gates, Alan Novidor, John Javna, Julie Bennett, D. Patrick Miller, Rick Fields; Jon Adolph, Jennifer King, Jeff Wagenheim, Dan Fields, Lisa Horvitz, and the rest of the *New Age Journal* staff; Doug Barasch of *Sesame Street Parents*. I don't quite know what I did to earn the friendship and support of such marvelous and gifted people, but I do know enough to be grateful for it.

My constitutional ecumenicism stems largely from my many years toiling in the vineyards with Michael and Justine Toms at New Dimensions Radio. I didn't first encounter Eastern religions through that work, but I certainly learned just how vast was the array of spiritual teachings available to a curious soul living in our time. Also, my work as a journalist has been shaped by my training in the New Dimensions School of Empathetic Interviewing, which holds that our interviewees, amazingly enough, are not our adversaries. That training, more than anything else, has enabled me to conduct conversations with scores of people, famous and not, in a way that leads both me and my subject to discover something of value for us and my readers. It's hard to imagine ever being able to come close to that if I hadn't had the good fortune of Michael and Justine's influence.

The families represented in this book opened their hearts and souls to me when I had no right to expect them to do so. Not only did they make it possible for me to do this book, they made it *necessary:* it was so frustrating trying to condense their stories into sidebars or squeeze them all into a single feature article, that I just *had* to write a book to do them justice. Still, they could have given me pithy quotes and been done with me, or guarded their privacy as jealously as any media-savvy citizen might do in this tabloid age; instead, they revealed intimate and often difficult truths about their experiences, and brought me ever closer to the heart of what it means to have a spiritual life. I bless them all.

My thinking has been influenced by a great variety of religious philosophers, spiritual teachers, artists, anthropologists, sociologists, social critics, psychologists, and sacred texts. A few deserve special mention: Matthew Fox, Huston Smith, Polly Berrien Berends, Jesus, the Buddha, St. Francis of Assisi, Pope John XXIII, Jean Grasso Fitzpatrick, J. Krishnamurti, Gandhi, Rumi, Martin Buber, Joseph Campbell, Angeles Arrien, Bobby McFerrin, Bruce Cockburn, David James Duncan, Buckminster Fuller, Gary Snyder, Wendell Berry, Wade Clark Roof, David Heller; the *Bhagavad-Gita,* the *Tao Te Ching,* the *Dhammapada, The River Why,* the *I Ching,* and yes, the Bible. Their impact on me ranges from the imperceptible to the obvious, and besides acknowledging my debt to them, I would like to obscure my own shortcomings with their reflected grandeur.

My parents, Dante Agosto Catalfo and Frances Alfano Catalfo, taught me from my earliest days that religion is at the center of human life, family identity, and community culture; through all my seemingly aimless spiritual wanderings, that lesson has always informed my course settings. Also, they first showed me what "faith" means by having faith in me, and I hope they feel now that it was not misplaced.

My wife and children let an erratic, moody, over-whelmed guy live with them for several months, without asking my permission . . . no, what I mean is, I wasn't always fun to be around in the final months of working on this book. And that was after several years' worth of interrogation, as I used them as experimental subjects and raw material for my writing (what else is new?), dragging them off to various churches and chant-a-thons and other only-Dad-coulda-thought-of-this events, trying various prayers and rituals on for size, and just generally making a nuisance of myself with The Whole Spirituality Thing. It would have been enough for them just to love me, or even just to let me eat and sleep there and pick up my mail and do my laundry. That they shared my excitement and adventure, nagged and encouraged me, allowed me to pursue my own personal Holy Grail, was surely more than I deserved. Sharing my life with them gives it meaning, which is lucky for me. I hereby humbly request permission to resume biting their cheeks, tickling their bellies, and just holding them in my arms forever and ever.

Contents

Contents

Introduction:
To the Further Shore

Few among men are they who cross to the further shore.
The others merely run up and down the bank on this side.
—Dhammapada: Sayings of the Buddha,
(translated by Walpola Rahula)

My religious life hasn't turned out quite like I once thought it would.

Thirty-odd years ago, I was a devout Catholic. I attended St. Aloysius Parochial School in Brooklyn, New York, serving in the parish church as an altar boy and even aspiring to the priesthood. In my neighborhood, deep in the heart of an Italian-American district near the Brooklyn-Queens border, it seemed the entire world was of Italian extraction and devoutly Catholic. Old-World-style *festas*, or festivals (like the one portrayed in the film *The Godfather, Part II*) in honor of saints' feast days, were still celebrated on our streets, which were closed for the occasion; the annual feast day of one's patron saint was only a bit less important than one's birthday.

Before the great postwar exodus to suburbia, someone born in such a locale would ordinarily be baptized, receive First Communion, be confirmed, marry, and be buried in the same church. However stifling that may seem to some today, a life so deeply intertwined with the liturgy and clergy and seasonal rites of the local house of worship at least offered a sense of continuity, and a kind of inherited spiritual practice, that many find hard to come by today, when many neighborhoods and even whole cities are barely a generation or two old. But that continuity proved elusive in my lifetime.

In 1962, when I was eleven, my family moved to San Diego. I went from parochial school to public school, and from a homogeneous, religious culture to a heterogeneous, secular one. Suddenly it became clear that the rest of the world was not only not Italian-American, or Catholic, or even Christian; it included people who actually *had no religion at all.* In California, too, there was a sybaritic spirit so pervasive, especially among the young, that it eclipsed even the festiveness of my Italian forebears—a sense of the rightness and availability of pleasure, of physical joy. Before long, my priestly aspirations had evaporated.

But it wasn't just an accident of geography that

caused the detour in my spiritual journey—and in fact, I didn't take the detour until I had first tried sticking to my original route. During my high school years, I began to test my faith, to insist that it be relevant to my emerging social consciousness and the political realities of the time. And I tried to determine once and for all if I really believed all the things I'd memorized from my Baltimore catechism: Was there a personifiable God (in whose "image and likeness" I was made)? Was Jesus His only begotten Son? Was mine the "one, true" church? Was there a Heaven and a Hell? If so, was this life really just a kind of airport in which souls make connections to one or the other final destination? Were we—was I—guilty of original sin?

The last question proved to be the kicker. Even without an exalted sense of myself, I just couldn't, no matter how hard I tried, bring myself to feel "originally" guilty. There was an appetite for the adventures and pleasures of this life brewing within me, and while I understood the imperative to lead an ethical life, I couldn't dismiss my curiosity and instinct as betraying a "baser" nature. Curiosity, a questioning intelligence, an eagerness to know the things life seemed to want to show me, a willingness to discover awkward or difficult or unorthodox truths—that *was* my nature.

By 1968, when I entered college, I had already been exposed, albeit perfunctorily, to Buddhism and Hinduism, but more significantly, I had stopped attending Mass, going to confession, or finding any reason at all to enter a Catholic church (even the rustic eighteenth-century mission where Junipero Serra preached, and where my youthful beliefs made their last stand). In short, I no longer identified myself as a Catholic. I became immersed in the social upheaval of the times, especially focused on the Vietnam War, and was less concerned with matters of spiritual philosophy than those of progressive politics, the counterculture, and as hedonistic a lifestyle as I dared to explore. The next time I got around to epistemology, it seemed to me that I no longer believed in God.

But by 1975, when, after a sojourn in Latin America, I resettled in the San Francisco Bay area, I was becoming attracted to the myriad of voices of an emerging contemporary spirituality that came to be called New Age. I read several volumes in Carlos Castaneda's possibly fictional account of his apprenticeship with a Yaqui shaman, and learned to use the ancient Chinese oracle, the *I Ching*. Through the early-to-mid-1970s, my partner Michelle and I encountered Tibetan Buddhist lamas and Hindu swamis; enrolled in (and "graduated" from) several weekend-long human-potential workshops; met French obstetricians promoting "birth without violence"; learned something about Bach Flower Essences (administering, with some success, one called "Rescue" to a beloved cat who had been attacked by several dogs); studied *T'ai Ch'i*; practiced small-scale organic farming; had "psychic readings" done by students at a local "psychic institute." Some things made more sense, and were more enduringly useful, than others, but we were curious about nearly everything, at least initially. And by following our own curiosity, we reinhabited our spirituality—without even realizing we were doing so.

During this time, I wasn't sure I believed in God in the same way I had as a Catholic schoolboy, but I was comfortable exploring these new ways to express my soul's questions; I was happy, in any case, to be dealing with matters of the soul, with or without the hard-and-fast answers that religious dogma offers. For, while leaving open the question of the existence of an all-knowing, all-seeing Supreme Being, I knew there was a part of me that hungered to know about such things, that gravitated toward a level of consciousness beyond ordinary bill-paying wakefulness, and that wouldn't go away no matter how much I ignored it. I had never been interested in focusing on what we now call the "inner life" to the exclusion of social-political-material awareness, but what this period of exploration taught me was that the converse wouldn't work either—I couldn't focus on the external to the exclusion of the internal, and still live a meaningful, useful, happy life.

Michelle and I married in 1978, and had our first child, Jessamine, a year later. Our first son, Gabriel, was born—at home—in 1983; our second, Peter, likewise in 1986. During those years, I worked for New Dimensions Radio, producer of the nationally syndicated program *New Dimensions*, which put me in touch with a ceaseless parade of spiritual teachers from every philosophical school on the planet, further "ecumenicizing" my religious point of view. For many years I identified with what *New Dimensions* host Michael Toms often said, only half-jokingly, about his own religious identity: "I'm a Christian Existentialist Vedantic Buddhist." (Today Michael would probably add a few denominations to the mix.) This was a spiritually-rich experience, and satisfied something very deep within me, even though I continued to settle on relatively few "certainties." (Reincarnation? Sin? Afterlife? These are ideas more easily considered than nailed down, especially when one is exposed to articulate proponents of divergent viewpoints in quick succession—or if one is open-minded enough to pursue an elusive truth over no-doubts-allowed doctrine.) But while it was enriching my inner life, it did not prepare me for a profound dilemma which the arrival of our children made inevitable.

Michelle, who had been raised in the Lutheran church, and I, were both loathe to raise our children within either of the faith traditions into which we had been born. It's safe to say that we were both comfortable with the essential teachings of Jesus as we understood them. But we were strongly disinclined to expect that our children believe much of what we were taught to accept without question when we were young—especially when we had our own differences with various doctrines and practices of modern institutionalized Christianity. (Lately, I have been wondering if my relationship with the Catholic church would have been much different if Pope John XXIII's successors had furthered his ecumenical work and helped carry forward his empathetic spirit, instead of taking the Church in a retrogressive direction. But that's like wondering what might have been if John F. Kennedy had lived, or if the Beatles had stayed together.)

We had no other religion or spiritual practice to put in place of the Lutheran and Catholic faiths or our childhoods, and we didn't *want* one. Neither of us had been to church regularly in ten years or more; wouldn't it be hypocritical to start attending now? Maybe it was best, in any case, not to direct our children's spiritual journeys, but to let them choose their own as they grew, following their hearts without the unnecessary burden of having to reconcile their own beliefs, questions, and doubts with a set of doctrines that would likely prove rigid and archaic. In the absence of choosing any particular way of spiritual child-rearing, we "chose" no way.

To her credit, Michelle questioned the wisdom of this course before I did. While our children were still babies it may not have mattered much, but as they grew through toddlerhood into actively inquisitive youngsters, fully engaged with the world around them, she noted that something seemed missing. As the kids began to acquire a familiarity with seasonal celebrations such as Easter, Thanksgiving, and Christmas (which we observed in a secular way), Michelle would lament the lack of a religious frame of reference with which the children could interpret these clearly important recurring events. Eventually it began to dawn on me, too. For one thing, without basic instruction, our children weren't conversant with even the most well-known Bible stories and the central lessons they taught. We realized that, even though we ourselves no longer believed in, say, the Immaculate Conception, or Resurrection, or took the story of the birth in the manger literally, there was still a certain comfort, and valuable memories, to be had in recalling the Gospel accounts at those special times of the year. Whatever else they might find on their own, our children would not have that comfort, or reflect back as adults on what those stories had meant to them in their youth. These were stories and beliefs that had been passed on for countless generations in both our families. Even though we did not want to pass them on as *our* beliefs, we were saddened to realize that we ourselves were the point at which the legacy was not being transmitted—the point past which the circle would no longer be unbroken. (I have similar regrets, incidentally, about the fact that my kids are growing up in a home in which Italian is not spoken.)

But if that realization made us wistful, it was not a pressing problem. There was, however, another repercussion to our family's lack of a tangible spiritual practice that was more troubling. It had to do with what our children were showing they needed from us, and from our life as a family, that we were not providing.

I remember when I first became aware that we had left Something Major untended. One day when Jessamine was about three years old, she was quite unself-consciously telling me a story of her own invention. The details of the story have been long since lost to me. All I remember is that somewhere in the course of telling it, she referred, in passing, to God. *Hmmm,* I thought. *I don't think we've ever even mentioned God to her, let alone taught her anything about God. I wonder where she got it from? I wonder what she means by it?* It was all I could do to wait for her to finish her story before asking her to tell me more about God. Who was God, to her?

She looked up at the ceiling for a moment, and then at me. And then, after the briefest pause, she said quietly but dramatically, "God is . . . *the unicorn of the mind.*"

If I had had a coherent thought at that point, I'm sure I would have been unable to utter it. I was, to use the vernacular, transported. Jessamine's words were not only sublimely lyrical in that out-of-the-mouths-of-babes way young children have, but also profound. I had spent nearly half my life sorting through various definitions of God, and here my own child had come up with a five-word version replete with meaning. To this preschooler, God was a magical, beneficent being; the epitome of beauty; an object of the heart's longing. In Jessamine's universe, that was a pretty comprehensive summation of the Divine, all right.

But when my rapture subsided, I realized that Jessamine had been conjecturing on Big Questions, posing some answers, piecing together her own cosmology—without any support from her parents. The good news was, she was doing this work on her own. The bad news was, she was doing this work on her own.

As the above anecdote—or any of a hundred most parents could offer—demonstrates, children will find their own entry into the Mystery, with or without their parents, and my own kids' curiosity about religious matters certainly hasn't been stifled by their lack of religious instruction. Jessamine's wondrous utterance was followed over the years by such milestones as Gabriel's offhanded comment that he had seen angels on several occasions, and Peter's terrifying realization (at age four, in mid-bath) that everyone dies eventually. All three have mused aloud or asked us directly about how the Universe is put together, tried to imagine the implications of having never been born, or reconciled themselves to the death of the pet because, as Gabe put it when he was little, "That's okay, he'll come back to life in another form." Clearly, the process of discovering the spiritual side of life is alive in them, and has been at least since they could speak. But, it turns out, children need their parents' help in that process just as surely as they do when they're learning to walk. I now believe that, among other things, parents are spiritual gardeners, and it falls to us to cultivate the ground in which our children's spiritual beliefs take root. Looking back on the choice Michelle and I made many years ago, it seems that our reluctance to force-feed our children any religion translated into no feeding at all.

And yet . . . there was no denying the reasons why we had elected not to assign ourselves a particular religion just so our kids would have a religious identity. We weren't Catholic, or Lutheran, or Buddhist, or Hindu. We were *spiritual*, not religious. Our beliefs were general and fluid, not specific, doctrinal, and fixed. Even in midlife we continue to struggle with fundamental spiritual questions. Even if we had agreed that we wanted to have a spiritual program for the sake of our kids, what would it be?

It's one thing, we were learning, to spend ten or twenty years—or an entire lifetime—plotting your own spiritual coordinates; it's quite another to have several spiritually voracious creatures biting on your ankles, wanting to know all about "Life, the Universe, and Everything" (as Douglas Adams put it), and not being especially eager to hear that you haven't sorted it all out yet. I came to see spiritual childrearing as the most awesome, perplexing, and unexpected responsibility of contemporary parenthood.

For millions of American parents today, my family's journey has a familiar ring to it. Of the seventy-five

million men and women born between 1946 and
1964—the "baby boomers"—fully two-thirds, according to recent sociological studies, left the faith
traditions in which they were raised by the time they
entered adulthood. Many dabbled in, or even became
serious students of, Eastern religions. Some became
devotees of arcane, even controversial spiritual teachers. Others seemed to have abandoned religion alto-
gether. But about half of all these "refugees"
eventually settled on a particular spiritual path, many
returning to their original denominations or choosing ones very similar. Among the most significant cat-
alysts in returning to regular worship or settling on a
single practice after extended periods of searching or
living an areligious lifestyle, are marriage and having
children.

There are at least two historic moments within this
generation's spiritual odyssey. First, religion became
a matter of choice, including the choice not to have
a religion at all. And second, after extensive experi-
mentation, searching, questioning, and often painful
apprehension of spiritual needs, millions of American
families began making unprecedented choices about
their spiritual lives and what kinds of practices best
suited them. Some opted out of the religious life—
that is, some chose, as Michelle and I did, not to provide any particular spiritual training or framework for

their children (some, of course, are agnostics or atheists). Some became part of the modern era's still-
burgeoning (and, to this writer, quite frightening)
fundamentalist movement, or found some other tradition hospitable. Others evinced the same kind of
adventurousness in their family's spiritual search that
they had brought to their own individual search, con-
cocting unique combinations of various religious philosophies or otherwise adhering to some form of what
one pundit called "roll-your-own religion." Still others—in great numbers, to judge by my own investigations—are still grappling with the kind of dilemma
I have described as my own. (We'll see what recent
research tells us about this generation's religious beliefs and patterns in Chapter One.)

I will not attempt to catalogue here the myriad ways
in which American spirituality takes form. Nor will I
attempt to document exhaustively all the things contemporary families are doing to give voice to their
spiritual selves—although we will see a fascinating
and characteristic sample. What *Raising Spiritual Children in a Material World* aims to do, instead, is to distill
the basic elements of the *process* of coming to terms
with one's spiritual life, as a seeker and a parent, with
an eye toward discovering and embarking upon the
appropriate spiritual path for one's family to walk together. We will encounter those elements as we meet

a selection of American families who have managed to establish thriving spiritual lives *as families,* and who share with us the lessons they've learned (sometimes painful, sometimes exultant, always deeply affecting) and the treasures they've found in the course of walking their paths. It is my fervent hope that their stories and the insights we acquire along the way will guide other families in their search for the right spiritual trajectory—and, in some cases, to inspire readers to believe, where they may not have been able to believe before, that it *is* in fact possible to develop a family practice that strengthens the bonds between members and nurtures all in their spiritual unfoldment.

Before we begin in earnest, I feel I owe you a bit more information about my own religious beliefs— that is, where I plot my own spiritual coordinates— and additional background about how this book came to be, both out of fairness to you, and because both elements figure notably in the aim and tone of this book.

As I amble through my fifth decade, watching my children grow, I continue to grapple with all the Big Questions I've been gnawing at all along; if anything, the certainties I thought I had pocketed in my youth and early adult years seem, more often than not, to have evaporated. But I think it's fair to say that, while

I subscribe to little in the way of formal doctrine (whether learned from the Catholic church in which I was baptized and raised, or encountered in any of the various religions I have studied over the years), there are some things I believe, and some other concepts I feel personally comfortable with even as I continue to discover their implications.

I no longer believe in the anthropomorphic God I envisioned as a child, but I do believe there is a Source for the universe in which we find ourselves—an Intelligence, if you will, or a Force; Buckminster Fuller called it Universe, in an effort to make the concept as expansive as possible. (My favorite Bucky Fuller quote: "You never hear Universe say, 'I'm not ready.' Universe never says, 'I don't know what to do about that.' ") While the policies of this Source may not always be discernible—as one friend of mine replied when I playfully asked him, quite suddenly one day, if there was a God, "Why yes, but his intentions remain unclear"—I think any parent who has beheld the face of her or his child would have a hard time disagreeing with the idea that, as I like to put it, "a lot of *thought* went into that." And you don't have to be a parent to feel yourself enveloped in and blessed by the ceaseless processes and everyday miracles of nature, which, while they *could* have developed quite by chance, would have had to surmount essentially impossible odds to do so. In other words, All This didn't have to happen, but it did; whether Somebody Up There instigated it or not, we are blessed that it did happen.

I don't mean to be coy here; I'm probably accurately described as an agnostic much of the time, at least when my outlook is compared with the more orthodox views I held earlier in my life. But one thing I've learned, which I find is particularly salient in today's world, is that *one need not be an adherent of a particular religious doctrine in order to find the sacred in life, or indeed to have a spiritually fulfilling life.* To be sure, it is harder, when one doesn't have a specific doctrine to hold on to, to sort out issues of belief and morality. But belief is not purchased over the counter; it is born of experience, trial and error, and the supremely difficult ordeal of being honest and open about what one finds both within one's heart and in the world outside. For me, at this stage of my life, it is enough that I can enjoy the sacrament of my children's smiles, that I can respect my fellow human beings as expressions of the same mysterious Source that brought my consciousness into being, that I can give thanks (without knowing precisely where to address them) for rain and sunshine and photosynthesis and reproduction.

I have tried, throughout this book, to maintain an

open, nonjudgmental stance toward the various spiritual practices examined here, and as broad a view of the landscape as possible. I did that because I felt the subject matter demanded it—and because I believe, in a time when we are seeing more and more murders committed in the name of religious belief, both in our own country and around the world, that our children's future depends on our being able to nurture tolerance and understanding. But I came to that view because I have found it to work for me in my own spiritual search, where close-mindedness, using belief as insulation against experience, and desperate dogmatism have definitely *not* worked to further my spiritual growth.

I could probably be accused of playing fast and loose with the word "God" in these pages. However, even though in my heart I do not believe in the Abrahamic God of the flowing white beard, I find the name we give to the ineffable to be more and more welcome on my lips and in my mind. Words are shorthand, after all, for the ideas and experiences they attempt to convey. In recognition of this, the ancient Hebrews had a taboo against using God's name, so inadequate was the word for the eternal Being they worshipped. But in today's ever more perplexing world, the word "God"—not the Deity or Source him/her/itself, but the term—is, at least for this seeker, a perfectly good metaphor and teaching tool (for myself and my family). Others may mean something quite specific and immutable when they utter God's name. In my case, every time I mention God I am reminding myself that I was born, live, and will die amid a Mystery that I don't expect to fathom fully until after my time here is done. And, I believe, when I use that term with my children, I am invoking something as deep as their souls—in other words, I am inviting them to embrace that Mystery. (The way I see it, they might as well get comfortable with it early!) In this book I have tried to use the word "God" in a way that recognizes that every child born is a gift from the Source; hopefully my usage will also remind us parents that reaching adulthood does not mean *we* are no longer "children" of that Source. To the extent that we can remember this, can work with it, the spiritual lives of our families will be richer.

In recent years my wife and I have searched for a more concrete way to express and pursue our spiritual selves with our children. We have visited various churches, encountered various clergy, and experienced a variety of worship services, sometimes with our children and sometimes alone. I had thought, when I began this book, that "finishing" that search was more or less a requisite of finishing the book.

However, I now see that idea as contrived, and am grateful that our search is not over: concluding it just to be tidy here would have been a disservice both to you and to our family; and, more importantly, the point was not to *conclude* the search but to *begin* it. However long it takes, we have already learned many important lessons about what we need, what kind of congregation and services are appropriate for us, and what kind of congregants we make. (I'll share some of our experiences, including what I find the most appealing service I've yet encountered, the "Planetary Mass," later.)

There is another dimension to the spiritual quest my family and I have been on in recent years that is important to acknowledge here. In the beginning of 1991, our son Gabriel, then seven, was diagnosed with a life-threatening illness—acute leukemia, the most common cancer among children. Ever since then, every aspect of our life as a family has been affected by this central fact, including (*especially*) our spirituality. Over the past six years we have been through triumph and setback, grief and hope, shattering heartache and boundless gratitude. Thankfully, his prognosis is good, although he has had to endure extremely arduous treatment to win a chance at a healthy future.

The reason I bring up our struggle with Gabe's illness is that it thrust us even more dramatically into a nose-to-nose confrontation with many of the spiritual questions that most of us (myself included) would rather handle abstractly: How can God do this to an innocent child? Will God save my son? What powers are available to me in this time of abject need? What possible meaning can this have? What possible justice can there be in this? Who did this? WHY? And because, through the desperation, fear, and pain this saga has brought us, we have learned again to use some spiritual tools which had been rusting in our souls' workshop.

Not surprisingly, primary among those tools is prayer. It's not true that I had never prayed in my adult life before Gabe got sick, but it was extremely rare for me to do so. Oh, I had consulted the *I Ching*, and meditated, and tried to focus energy and concentrate intention. But I seldom *prayed*. For one thing, things had generally gone pretty well in my life. (I wonder if God finds most humans like the boy who never utters a word until, at age ten or so, he suddenly declaims, "The cereal's cold," and who, when his amazed mother—having believed him to be mute—tearfully asks him why he hadn't spoken previously, says simply, "Up to now, everything was okay.") Moreover, I felt like it was my responsibility to handle pretty much whatever came along, without requisitioning any Help From Above.

Such a policy, of course, can make life hellish when you *do* need help. I began to view things differently some years ago when I heard the late Sun Bear, a Native American astrologer and New Age teacher, say, on a *New Dimensions* program, that it was *okay* to ask for help. Of course, many indigenous peoples have known since time immemorial that food doesn't grow out of the earth without essential assistance from some transcendent force that turns water and minerals and sunlight into substances that just happen to sustain our bodies. But we industrialized folks, burdened with a mistaken sense of our unlimited cleverness, seem to have a harder time relating to transcendent forces we can't look in the eye and grab with our hands, or in any case thinking we might need to turn to such forces. That was certainly true for me before I became a parent.

My position had softened some before Gabe got sick, but I leapt across a kind of chasm when I learned that his life was in danger. The day after the diagnosis, when I returned to the hospital where Michelle had spent the night with him, he was in a procedure room, sedated; when, a few minutes later, he was carried in and placed on his bed, still asleep, I found myself up to my ears in imploring those transcendent forces: I fell to my knees and cried, *"I call upon the powers of the universe to heal this boy!"* I can't tell you how I knew to do that, or figured out what to say. Somewhere in me the thought occurred, *Ask for help.* Desperate, in shock, I instinctively prayed.

Since that day, I have surely offered more prayers—of desire, hope, and gratitude—than in all the other years of my life; and they have definitely been more fervent than any I'd offered before. I've also learned a lot about how and why I pray: to maintain contact with the Mystery; to remain humble and keep seeking deeper understanding. Sometimes, of course, I pray in hopes of receiving a specific boon, ranging from guidance to employment to my children's well-being—I'm asking for help. But more and more, I pray because it is good to pray. Or, as C. S. Lewis said (in *Shadowlands*): "I don't pray because it changes God. I pray because it changes *me.*"

We'll examine prayer at greater length later in this book. I just wanted to come clean, so to speak, so that you could have a sense of just who you're talking to, at the outset.

There is another sense in which the forceful spiritual awakening that resulted from Gabe's illness led me to do this book; I'll explain that in Chapter One. Let me conclude this Introduction with a brief word on how *Raising Spiritual Children in a Material World* is organized.

This book has three basic elements. The first part, which includes Chapter One, is a broad overview of the peculiar circumstance in which many families find themselves today, as defined in recent sociological research, as well as my own investigations and experiences and those of people I've interviewed.

In the second part, Chapters Two through Six, we meet a series of families whose stories and spiritual practices illuminate, and offer inspiration and hope for, the predicament of wanting your family's spirituality to have more tangible form but not being sure which of the forms in the spiritual marketplace is best. I've organized these families and their stories around the kinds of needs and issues they were dealing with and the benefits they were accruing from their practices, so the reader can look for issues and solutions that parallel her or his own condition.

The third part of this book, chapters Seven through Nine, offers a compendium of thoughts, tools, prayers, and notes to help the contemporary family define and pursue its own spiritual practice. Chapter Seven, "Notes Along the Path," contains tips and reflections accumulated in the course of examining other families' spiritual odysseys, as well as advice on how to approach such blockbuster issues as talking about God with your children and the role of prayer. Chapter Eight, "Cairns in the Forest," shares my notes on my family's quest, and my own. Chapter Nine offers reflections on what it will take for our children to be able to lead healthy spiritual lives and have a healthy world to live them in.

A word about the title. The phrase "raising spiritual children" suggests that the focus of the discussion is on the children themselves: what we do about, for, and *to* them. However, it will quickly become apparent that the focus here is on parents: what we do about, for, and to ourselves, as spiritual beings, in the context of our role as parents. There are no recipes here for "producing" a "spiritual" child. None are necessary, for children, I'm not the first to point out, are intrinsically spiritual; but even if they were necessary, and even if I'd concocted them, I doubt I'd have included them. I'm not interested in a kind of benign behavior-modification program. I'm interested in what it takes for us to be the kind of parents we need to be in order to provide the most wholesome and spiritually rich home in which our children's souls might unfold.

What's more, I was after something more than glib

irony with the phrase "spiritual children in a material world." What I hoped to convey was several levels of meaning wrapped up in the problem of spiritual childrearing in today's society. The title of this book represents the duality confronting the parent, as indeed every human: the existential paradox of being an embodied soul in a physical realm. As parents, we want to be sure to nourish both facets—the physical and the spiritual—of the precious beings entrusted to our care. But the resolution of that paradox is not what it may appear to be at first.

On the one hand, many of us, whatever our political opinions or religious beliefs, worry about the runaway commercialization of society, the despiritualizing of modern life. Some people talk about this as a lack of "family values," as if people could have families and not have values. I think of it as an erosion of *human* values, in which the corporate engines of society have established the primacy of their own values and everything else has fallen by the wayside. In any case, we worry about the dehumanized culture our children are growing up in, and may seek to provide a more spiritual sensibility for them, as a kind of innoculation against the encroachment of the culture at large. For some people, then, "raising spiritual children in a material world" likely means, in a sense, *removing* them from that world: creating a controlled, hermetic environment in which to impart preferable values and beliefs.

And yet, we are bound to live, with our children, in a material, i.e., secular, world: we go to jobs, have transactions with merchants, observe the consequences of civil laws, set our clocks, and otherwise move through a realm of diverse beliefs and interests. I do not believe we should try to change that, in the sense of remaking the world to be more "spiritual"— and certainly not homogenously so. Today it's possible to, for example, watch all-Christian television channels (including Christian sitcoms and even *home shopping programs!*), read only Christian publications, visit Christian theme parks, work in Christian enterprises, and send your children to Christian schools. Of course, there's nothing "wrong" with that, and people should remain free to do so. However, I believe that monoculture is inimical to life. That's certainly true in ecosystems, and it's no less true in society, let alone in the world of the spirit. Our objective should instead be to *reinspirit* our individual and collective lives, indeed the commons itself, without lessening the secular center of gravity a polyglot, religiously diverse, multicultural world must have in order to function.

The aim of this book, then, is to discover how we can infuse our role as parents with an enlivened spirituality, and therefore be able to raise ''spiritual'' children, *while remaining* **in** the material world where our journey will be carried out.

I'm not a theologian; I'm not a born-again Christian; I'm nobody special, someone without enough doctrinal beliefs to frame in a stained-glass window. But, like the rest of us, I am trying, as the Buddha exhorted his followers to do, to work out my own salvation, and sincerely believe that my struggle to do just that will aid my children in their own efforts to do the same. The things I've learned from other families as well as authors, clergy, and teachers I've encountered, are just too good to keep to myself. So I offer them to you, humbly, and in appreciation of the difficulty and adventure that awaits us as we take one step after another—as individuals, as parents, and as families—on this journey we seem to be taking together.

CHAPTER 1
A Familiar Quest

*Inside the Great Mystery that is,
we don't really own anything.
What is this competition we feel, then,
before we go, one at a time, through the same gate?*
—Rumi
(translated by John Moyne and Coleman Barks)

In 1991, a few months after Gabe was diagnosed and began treatment, I happened to begin a series of conversations with my colleague Peggy Taylor, editor (and cofounder) of *New Age Journal (NAJ)*, about the spirituality of contemporary families, especially among our "baby boomer" generation. My particular interest in the subject at that time stemmed from the experiences I was having—learning to pray again; learning to ask *others* to pray on behalf of my son and my family; struggling to comprehend the fact that dozens, hundreds, thousands of people (including entire congregations of strangers) were praying for us; and wrestling, in a much more visceral way than ever before, with those Big Questions. In ways I could never have anticipated, the pain and difficulties my family and I were enduring opened me to my own spiritual life more deeply than ever before, and I was learning, through my own struggle and the examples of other families, how spiritual beliefs sustain a person, a family, and a community, especially in crisis. And, conversely, how the absence of a well-defined set of beliefs, and ways to give them form, can be a hindrance to one's effort to dig down deep to find extra strength or resolve. All this sharpened the dilemma which I spoke of earlier—the yearning for a spiritual practice for my family that would nourish our souls without compromising our autonomy or requiring us to fall back on dogma we had consciously disavowed.

Peggy, whose work over the past two decades has familiarized her with spiritual teachings and practices of virtually every stripe, and I were convinced that there were hundreds of thousands, even millions, of people in our generation who were grappling with a similar dilemma. We felt that their efforts to find the appropriate vehicle for their individual and family searches were giving rise to the amazing proliferation of spiritual schools, workshops, communities, and rituals which have dotted the religious landscape in recent years. It was of course no secret that legions of baby boomers had taken a meandering spiritual path, but we felt there was another dimension to that phenomenon that was going unappreciated, not to say unreported, amid the larger culture's tendency to marginalize new religious hybrids and spiritual experiments, and focus on trends in mainstream religion.

We wanted a way to tell that story, and it seemed that the story was best told by families themselves. Peggy suggested that we publish a reader survey—invite our readers to describe their religious background and spiritual practices—and assigned me the task of composing the survey. My enthusiasm for the subject got me past any reservations I had about not being qualified to craft a research instrument, and by keeping to the elements we had discussed (background, belief, rituals, learning, and teaching), I was able to come up with a series of thirty-five questions that prompted respondents to compile a sort of thumbnail spiritual autobiography. The survey, "Spirituality and the Family," was published in the September/October 1991 issue.

Family Portrait of a Generation

Before that issue left the newsstands, some 350 readers had completed the questionnaire and mailed it to us. There was great variety among the respondents' beliefs and practices, but one thing virtually all of them shared was passion. It often seemed, reading their responses, that they had waited their entire lives to be asked about their innermost beliefs, how they arrived at them, how they expressed them, how they passed them on to their children. Some didn't confine themselves to a "thumbnail" self-portrait: more than a few enclosed highly personal letters, even ten-to-twenty page essays. Taken as a whole, the survey response confirmed what Peggy and I suspected: that a significant number of American families were actively engaged in working out unique, almost customized, ways of meeting their spiritual needs; that our readership was characterized, in matters spiritual, by a constitutional aversion to dogma; that spiritual hunger in America had led to a vast array of spiritual agriculture, in which individuals, families, and communities were devising innumerable new ways to seek, approach, and worship the ineffable; and that, in many households, family spirituality had become a very different thing from what it had been only a generation earlier.

The survey results were tabulated by one of the magazine's editors and published in the magazine's July/August 1992 issue. I contacted about a dozen of the families who had responded and conducted lengthy interviews with them for profiles to accompany the survey results. Several of those families are represented here, along with a few others I have encountered along the way. The families you will meet include:

- A growing young Neopagan family in a small town on California's north coast;
- A family living in the Sierra Nevada foothills, who study the anthroposophy of Rudolf Steiner;
- A Knoxville, Tennessee, couple who practice a little-known meditation method from Japan;
- An Omaha family who have not only maintained, but deepened, the observance of Jewish ritual which they knew in their early lives;
- An African-American family in Boston's inner city, who practice a combination of Christian and African spiritual teachings, as a reflection of their cultural identity;
- A Westchester County, New York, couple who combine Judaism and Vedanta;
- The head of a Washington, D.C., nonprofit organization, who converted to Catholicism after having been raised in an areligious home, and his actress-playwright wife, who inclines to a Native American spiritual tradition; and
- An American-born Zen priest, spiritual director

of a Seattle-area meditation center, his Vietnamese-born wife, and their children, living a Buddhist lifestyle in a predominantly Judeo-Christian milieu.

I chose families not just for their spiritual diversity, which comprises a fascinating panoply of contemporary faith, but more importantly for the range of issues and needs that led them to their various practices, the different ways they formulated cultural and religious identity, and the myriad benefits the families have derived from their respective practices. Spirituality is not, in the end, something we can stage-manage or confine to one corner of our lives: it is at the center of our being, no matter how "spiritual" or "unspiritual" we see ourselves, and touches every aspect of human experience, as these families show. Getting to know these families, being invited by them to look into their most intimate beliefs, convinced me that families who want to discover an authentic spirituality, but don't know how to do it, need not feel the task is beyond their ken—no matter how lost or unrooted they may feel, how "rusty" they are, how trapped in their own logic they are, how "late" they are to begin their search, how intractable their pain or bewilderment. *These people found a way*, I thought, *and so can I.* And so can you.

It should be said that this cannot be considered a scientific survey—for one thing, the respondents were self-selecting—and we must be careful not to make too much of these results. The *NAJ* readership is clearly spiritually minded, and we can figure that those who took the time and effort to compose extensive, articulate responses cared more than even the average *NAJ* reader about these matters. But no matter how we try to downplay their fervor or discount their numbers, what emerges from the tabulations is a clear image of a notable segment of the American adult popluation that will not be told what to believe, choosing instead to forge its own beliefs and expressions in its own way and in its own time:

- Of the respondents, 60 percent identified their households as "nuclear" families, 12 percent as "extended," and 23 percent as single-parent; they had an average of 1.7 children. Nearly four-fifths, 78 percent, said they believed in God; 95 percent of those who said they didn't believe in God nonetheless reported they believed in "something"; virtually *none* called themselves atheists.
- Two-thirds of our respondents were raised by parents who both came from the same faith, and only 14 percent were exposed as children to re-

ligious teachings outside the Judeo-Christian tradition—and yet 95 percent said they had, in the
years since, investigated other spiritual philosophies, and 62 percent had followed a "spiritual
teacher" at one time or another (some, obviously, continue to do so).

- Only about 30 percent of respondents said they
maintained a relationship with the faith traditions
of their youth. Most had been raised Protestant
(Methodist, Presbyterian, Episcopalian, Lutheran, Baptist, and the like), but only 11 percent
of those still adhered to their childhood denominations. Only 25 percent of those raised Catholic
remained in the church. By and large, respondents had replaced their childhood religions with
practices that allowed them vastly more room to
move: Pagan, Unitarian, non-denominational
Christian, Buddhist, "metaphysical," "spiritual."
The most popular answer to the question "What
religion do you practice?" Was "None."

- Our respondents nonetheless seemed keenly
aware of and open to the metaphysically unpredictable. Some 84 percent said they had had "unusual spiritual experiences." They were also open
about these experiences: 79 percent said they had
discussed them with their children.

- Almost nine out of ten respondents—88 percent—reported that they prayed, and 72 percent said their children prayed. The most popular ritual was grace at mealtimes.

- Two-thirds of our respondents said they provide their children with religious training; 92 percent talk with their kids about God; 80 percent said they were satisfied with their ability to discuss spiritual matters with their children; and 70 percent said their children showed an interest in spiritual matters.

Having developed this snapshot of one portion of a leading-edge magazine's readership, we have to ask ourselves how well that snapshot fits with a more considered portrait of a larger population sample. And the answer, as it turns out, is: rather well.

Finding Our Own Way

The results of the homegrown *NAJ* survey tie in neatly with what recent sociological research tells us about religious patterns among the one-third of the American population known as "baby boomers"—the seventy-six-million-strong cohort born between 1946 and 1964. In his 1993 book *A Generation of Seekers: The Spiritual Journeys of the Baby Boom Generation*, sociologist Wade Clark Roof, professor of religion at the University of California, Santa Barbara, reported the results of what he called "the first large-scale study of boomers' spiritual lives," which he conducted in 1988–89.

The study contacted more than 2,600 randomly-selected households in four states, finding one boomer-age individual per household. These respondents consented to twenty-minute phone interviews during which they were asked eighty questions about their background, religious practices, moral values, and the like. More than 500 were contacted again later for follow-up interviews, in which fifty additional, more probing questions were asked. This research led Roof to the following conclusions about baby-boomers' religious attitudes and habits:

- The generation could be divided into four discrete types: **Loyalists** (33 percent), who never left the religious fold into which they were born; **Returnees** (25 percent), who dropped out of their childhood congregations but came back, most often upon becoming parents; **Believers-but-Not-Belongers** (28 percent), who "have little or no contact with organized religion yet say they are religious or spiritual"; and **Seekers** (9 percent), for whom "life is an adventure that leads to discoveries and insights that can flow only from their own experiences."

- Two-thirds, then—everyone but the Loyalists—of all boomers with religious backgrounds dropped out of church or synagogue by the time they reached adulthood.
- More than half—60 percent—of all boomers believe "it is better to explore the teachings of various religions than to stick with a particular faith."
- A whopping 80 percent believe it is possible to be a good Christian without attending church; 60 percent "think 'people have God within them, so places of worship are not really necessary.' "
- Fully three-forths of all boomers favor the ordination of women clergy.

Roof's interpretive analysis of the results of his research was also quite interesting, and correlated well with what the *NAJ* respondents demonstrated. "The boomers are broadening the range of activities normally associated with spiritual concerns," he wrote in *USA Today.* Given "its interest in moving beyond self and relating one's life to a larger order, we can expect a continuing, flourishing spirituality. Boomers' quests run too deep and too broad to be easily abandoned." Given the generation's trendsetting position in American life, it was not surprising that "religion in this country is in a time of transformation." As he noted in his book, "members of this generation are asking questions about the meaning of their lives, about what they want for themselves and for their children. They are still exploring, as they did in their years growing up; but now they are exploring in new, and, we think, more profound ways."

Thus, the quest on which I found myself, which the *NAJ* readers were clearly on as well, turned out to be a familiar quest for most of our generation. We were seeking a format for our spiritual lives that not only didn't ignore our political values—which were, generally speaking, more progressive than those of previous generations—but also integrated them fully. We longed for spiritual understanding arrived at honestly—that is, we were willing to study no end of religious teachings, but we didn't want to be told what to think or believe. We would not adhere to doctrines—no matter how central to our churches—we could not in good conscience accept, if they contradicted our own personal beliefs on such issues as womens' rights and reproductive rights, the separation of church and state, and sexual preference. We were less inclined to accept any one faith's teachings as the only valid ones, learning instead to recognize spiritual wisdom from various of the world's religious traditions. In short, we insisted on finding our own way.

Roof points out in his book that boomers "came of age in a time of increased choices and optimistic dreams," and has written elsewhere that, where previous generations took their religious participation for granted, boomers see religion as a matter of "calculated choice," including the choice not to practice any religion at all. It can be argued that the boomers' self-directed approach to such weighty matters owes to the relative affluence of the circumstances into which they were born—that, in terms of pioneering humanistic psychologist Abraham Maslow's "hierarchy of needs," they were the first generation whose material needs were so well taken care of that they had the luxury of attending to religious matters with such an autonomous attitude. That may be true, but I think there is something larger at work here than good fortune—or, at least, that good fortune has positioned this generation to accomplish something unprecedented in the history of human spiritual endeavor.

I believe that, after two millennia in which the Judeo-Christian tradition has shaped the Western mind, something more variegated, more ecumenical, is taking root in our religious sensibility. It is informed, to be sure, by extensive contact with Eastern religions, but that is not all. What we are witnessing has more to do with an openness, even a restlessness, of spirit, than the particular teachings to which an individual or a generation may be attracted. In significant numbers, today's spiritual pilgrims are giving birth to a post-denominational spirituality—and not a moment too soon. From at least the days of Christian Rome, through the Dark Ages, through the feudal era, during the Islamic conquests, through the Crusades, throughout the colonization of the New World, all the way down to latter-day atrocities such as the Holocaust, the Serbian-led "ethnic cleansing" of Bosnian Muslims, and other modern horrors, institutionalized religion has been made an instrument of subjugation, oppression, even genocide. It is not overstating the case to consider that we have one last chance to transcend the kind of fanaticism, so often engendered by certain fundamentalists and other religious manipulators, which convinces us that "infidels" in our midst are worthy of extermination. Even in the post–Cold War world, as long as weapons of mass destruction remain available, we must overcome this deep-seated tendency to use our religious beliefs to justify hatred, or we risk our own demise. Whether we are consciously seeking it or not, the creation of new forms of spiritual expression, the turning away from the strictures of dogma and the confines of denominationalism, is, I believe, an attempt to do just that. If we are successful—and I believe we will be, although the full fruits of our efforts may not be borne until our children's generation matures—we may, ironically, rediscover what religion was created for in the first place.

What Is Religion For?

I often think about the early humans who left behind the first religious artifacts: the cave paintings and henges of neolithic Europe, the petroglyphs of the American southwest, totems and carvings and ceremonial adornments found among the ruins of ancient settlements around the world. I try to imagine what motivated them to create these images and objects, through which they still speak to us, in some cases, tens of thousands of years later. What prompted them to fashion brushes and pigments and invent religious art? What did *they* think they were doing? What were they saying to *themselves*, let alone us?

In my imagination, what they were saying goes something like this: *We were here. We shared this place with these other beings. They had some powers, and we had some powers. There was so much magic we didn't understand it all. There were spirits in the air, on the land, in the sea; everywhere, spirits. We think maybe we are spirits, too. We tried to understand just what we are. This is as far as we got.*

The first religious impulses in humans must have come from a sentiment very much like that. There were no "traditions" or doctrines to follow; somebody had to start. What would have made him or her do it? An encounter with the Mystery, an apprehension of self-consciousness, the first expression of that continuing need to understand and explain the peculiar circumstance in which humans find themselves. In that distant time, religion was not invented to control behavior or conquer territory or organize society; it was invented by early humans to help them make sense of their world! Religion, religious art, ritual—these were crucial first tools, devised by the species that distinguished itself from its forerunners by its tool-making ablity, to help it in the ongoing task of "learning to be human," as Jean Grasso Fitzpatrick puts it in her book *Something More*.

Here's what we have forgotten over the centuries, and are struggling to relearn: *This remains the primary purpose of religion*. In fact, it could be argued that this is the *only* valid and practical purpose of religion. Of course, religion has been used for other purposes: to dispel fear, control behavior, order society, justify political and military campaigns. But religion is not meant to be about *other* people's deeds, sins, salvation, or beliefs. Religion is the training ground, supply depot, and point of embarcation for *one's own* journey, for the lifelong task of tending one's spiritual self, for the ceaseless effort to achieve understanding, for finding out who you are and what you're doing here.

Having said that, how can we as parents provide our children with the support they need from us so that they can be equipped and motivated to begin their own spiritual journeys? Isn't there a contradiction here? In some sense, there is, and many parents, myself included, have found themselves at an impasse over precisely that paradox—if the spiritual journey is at its essence an individual one, how can anything I try to do to assist my child *not* get in her or his way? Again, my wife and I, and countless other parents of our generation, resolved that dilemma, when we began having children, by avoiding the imposition of a religious program—only to find, later on, that we had overlooked a crucial component of our responsibility as parents, not to mention an enriching aspect of family life. Now, after years of questioning and searching, many of us are coming to see that the paradox which stymied us back at the beginning of our parenting careers was really only the first level of grappling with the question of family spirituality.

For it is also true that, since humans first adopted spiritual practices, those practices have been handed down from generation to generation. Children were exposed from their earliest years to the rituals and cosmologies of their elders, and grew up knowing very clearly their people's understanding of the universe in which they found themselves. In story, dance, sacrifice, prayer, costume, hunting rituals, fertility rites, betrothal ceremonies, harvest songs, campfire gatherings, and myriad other ways, children, families, clans, villages, towns, and peoples created and enacted their state-of-the-art interpretations of who they were and how their world was put together. There was, we can imagine, little or no separation between the spiritual and the mundane: in preindustrial cultures, there was nothing to intervene between a person and a mystical encounter with his or her surroundings. Indeed, to this day, many indigenous peoples, especially those few whose lives are relatively unaffected by modern technology, are known to "sing" into being their every act, their very world. I remember watching with fascination, a few years ago, a PBS documentary about a native people in a remote area of Alaska. At one point, two women were waiting for the arrival of a plane which would take them on to their destination. The plane was late, and as their wait got longer and longer, they took to chanting spontaneously-composed songs that exhorted the plane to arrive. When it finally came, they were sure— or at least, joked—that their songs had brought the plane. If that's not a pervasive sense of the spiritual,

I don't know what is. And I think that any parent concerned about cultivating spirituality in their children will find much food for thought in the spiritual attitude of certain cultures whose religious practices and lore have changed little since they first evolved, generations, centuries, even millennia ago.

If the religious impulse hasn't changed much since it first arose in humans, our overall psychological and spiritual makeup hasn't either. We are still born helpless, defenseless, ignorant—pure capacity, nothing but potential. Our needs have to be met by others. We must be educated in the ways of the world, especially our local universe. We have instincts, of course, and our brains and bodies are marvelously designed and programmed to grow and unfold to support our continued flowering, our growing into mature, self-reliant, successful beings. But we require instruction, or, at our earliest developmental stages, "imprinting," in order to engage fully with the complex processes that will see us to that point.

The work of child psychiatrist Robert Coles, to name just one distinguished body of research, has shown that children need to feel connected to something larger, need to have a sense of the spiritual. I would argue that they're "built" that way—that humans are designed to inquire, to contemplate the abstract, to apprehend the Mystery. And that the human condition virtually guarantees that they will. Our task as parents, then, becomes nurturing those facets of our children's personalities; encouraging and cajoling them as they begin to inquire, contemplate, and apprehend; and helping them develop the skills, attitudes, and training they will need to have under their belts in order to deal with that side of life fruitfully and attain a kind of spiritual "fitness." (*Not* correctness, but well-being, balance, self-reliance.) Let us say that, ideally, our spiritual childrearing would be no different from its material equivalent—that we would aim to provide our children with the education, guidance, and resources they will need to have integrated when their journey proceeds past the point where we can keep them under our protective wing. And, returning to the question posed earlier, we must not overlook one koan-like fact: we provide the spiritual support they need for their journey, not merely by *giving* them anything (as with food, clothing, shelter), but also by undertaking the journey ourselves.

What Is "Family Spirituality"?

Throughout this book, we will look at the individual and collective experience of spirituality. In particular, we will examine and define some of the many forms of spirituality as practiced by contemporary families, in hopes of arriving at a sense of what is most valuable and helpful, spiritually speaking, to families today. It would be useful to consider at this point what "family spirituality" means in the abstract, before we begin examining it in more minute detail.

A family is composed of individuals, of course, but the complex of relationships that make up a family result in a kind of organism in its own right, the synergistic by-product of all the interpersonal dynamics between parent and child, child and sibling, spouse and spouse. This happens at the social and psycho-emotional levels, and it's not too much to suggest that it happens at the spiritual level as well. For, when we consider the bonds among family members in all their dimensions, we can see that healthy family relationships mean love, support, guidance . . . and a sense of shared destiny. Spouses join their lives with the intention of sharing them "until death do us part"; biological relationships—between parent and child, and among siblings—are irrevocable. One thing we know about family relationships: they leave their mark upon us, not just on our psyches and in our hearts, but in our very souls. When you are talking about something so primal as the appearance of a child where there was none before, or the covenant between parents who conceive that child, or the bond between siblings who have been nurtured in the same womb, how can you *not* consider being a family as a spiritual experience?

Your Family Life *Is* Your Spiritual Practice. It may be most helpful, then, to think of the comingling of psyches that happens in families as being first and foremost a spiritual process. Whatever else we may *think* we're doing—chores, or paying bills, or transporting kids, or going on vacation, or watching TV— we are doing the spiritual work called "Being a Family." Many families, of course, adhere to a faith whose customs and tenets—including ritual, the attending of worship services, religious instruction, and so on— they identify as their spiritual practice. But we would do well to realize that, just as spirituality is not confined to certain hours of the day or days of the week, neither is spiritual work.

Eastern religions have a concept that speaks to this very well: *sadhana*. The *Shambhala Dictionary of Buddhism and Zen* says that this Sanskrit word is "derived from *sadh*, 'to arrive at the goal,' and meaning roughly 'means to completion or perfection.' " I have always taken *sadhana* to mean "soul work," i.e., the work of developing your soul toward enlightenment— or the *form* that that work takes. You can be a farmer, a priest, an artist, a nurse, a hospice worker, or a plumber; any of these vocations can be your *sadhana*, so long as you see your "job" in this way and engage in the process sincerely—as long as you do your *sadhana*. Every role in the world holds the promise of *sadhana*, and every being will eventually discover his or her *sadhana*. And so, our positions as parents (and, for that matter, as children and siblings), and our lives as families, can be, and in fact are, our *sadhana*, if we but choose to see things that way. Your family may identify itself as Catholic, Jewish, Hindu, or any other denomination under the sun (or none at all), but whatever congregation you may belong to, you are already members of the First Church of Family.

Having said that, the following questions arise: How do we recognize family spirituality? What forms does it take? Like anything else about being a family, the answers involve our doing things together.

Seeking Together. One way we can know we are doing the spiritual work of being a family is by striving to define what we're after: asking Big Questions and grappling with their answers; incorporating metaphysical dialogue into our everyday life as a family; and taking time to notice our own, and each other's, experiences, difficulties, confusion, and discussing them openly. In other words, by making our inner experience more apparent, our longings more evident, we make our spirituality more overt. Then it becomes another form of sustenance available to us, no less than the staples in the pantry or the perishables in the refrigerator. When someone in the family is hungry, they're likely to wander into the kitchen and rummage around for some food. They might even say out loud, "I'm *hungry!*" or "I could *really* go for some fruit/dessert/munchies/whatever!" So it is with our souls' hunger. By seeking out the food our souls need, together, we make family spirituality more palpable, both to ourselves and to our children.

Ritualizing Together. It will come as no surprise to anyone who's been a parent for more than a year or so that children, especially young children, love repetition and regularity. They want a certain game or story or activity to go a certain way, *every time.* The familiarity of these activities makes them feel secure, but I wonder how many of us stop to think that their penchant for repetition makes them natural-born ritualizers.

Ritual is what we do when we want to make a meta-statement about whatever's going on—a meal, a birthday, a wedding, or any of life's milestones, large and small. Perhaps children take to this so naturally because *everything* is a powerful experience for them. When was the last time you saw a blasé two-year-old? Unfortunately, most of us take more things for granted as we grow older, even before we "graduate" to adulthood; there are some seriously jaded twelve-year-olds running loose out there today (some of them are inhabiting forty-year-old bodies). Healthy, active ritualmaking in the family can help counteract ennui in our kids before it takes root.

By engaging in ritual as a family, we teach our children to honor the moment, cherish the day, and observe the seasons of life. By participating in rituals with our children, we teach *ourselves* to remain present, i.e., conscious, in the moment, and really be with our children, our spouses, ourselves. By creating new rituals together, we find that there is no limit to the ways in which our family's spirituality can manifest, and we invoke the Spirit in ourselves, to guide us and breathe life into our spiritual voices.

When I suggest creating new rituals, by the way, I don't mean that you have to craft something elaborate or protracted. You can if you want to—and if your kids' attention span holds out—but you can also come up with microrituals that can infuse your daily life with comfort and meaning and become signposts for each of you. For instance, one day when my daughter Jessamine was a toddler (back before the last ice age), she bade me good-bye with a cheery, "Have a lucky day!" It seemed like such a wonderful benediction that we immediately adopted it as our standard way to take our leave of each other. To this day, when someone leaves the house for work or school in the morning, we say, not, "Have a good day," but "Have a lucky day!" Now, we have had some good luck, and we've had some bad luck, in all the days we've been saying that. But we continue to say it, because it has become a family ritual, our way of wishing the best for each other, a kind of prayer for well-being and good fortune that reminds us how much we mean to each other.

Learning Together. Every day brings new lessons; every year they compound. Lessons we thought we had learned long ago resurface, to be reckoned with anew or more deeply. We can take pride in watching our children learn very tangible lessons as they grow, but we may forget that becoming a parent does not mean our learning has been completed. Spirituality is ultimately about learning how to move through life, how to become the person you were born to be; few among us have that nailed down.

Now, parents are called upon every day to be teachers, to instruct their children in the physical, emotional, and moral skills needed to make it in this world. And because parents bear the awesome responsibility of protecting and guiding their children, they must have authority to set the parameters for their children's lifestyle. But it does not lessen our authority, or make us any less the teacher, to remember that we also are learning, every day—how to be the best parents we can be; how to become the people we were born to be—and that in many respects our children are *our* best and wisest teachers. What's more, besides the lessons we teach each other, there are things we learn together from the world around us and the fact of living in it together.

Learning is at root a spiritual experience, because every bit of learning brings a further unfolding of the learner. So it is with families: as we learn, individually and together, we are proceeding down the spiritual path we embarked upon when we became a family. To promote the deepest learning, in ourselves and in our children, we should use the same tactics that work in a classroom: ask questions; don't be afraid to make mistakes; share what you know; engage in dialogue.

Sometimes, *what* we learn is not as important as *that* we learn. The lessons that life holds in store for us, and the ongoing process of integrating them, are the fuel that sustains the spiritual life of our family.

CHAPTER 2
"The Divine Nature of the Universe"

Up among the firs where it smells so sweet
or down in the valley where the river used to be
I got my mind on eternity
Some kind of ecstasy got a hold on me.
—Bruce Cockburn,
"Wondering Where the Lions Are"

"The most sacred thing in my life was always the natural world around me," says Anne Newkirk Niven, age thirty-six, of the northern California seaside town of Pt. Arena. Throughout her Christian upbringing in Tacoma, Niven recalls, she viewed the magic of nature—such as Washington's Mt. Rainier, which she could see from her bedroom window—in terms of "the language and consciousness of Christianity—'God's creation.'" Though she remained a Christian long enough to earn a Master of Divinity degree from the Pacific School of Religion in Berkeley, she abandoned her plans to become a Methodist minister, in part because she felt "somewhat disillusioned about the opportunities for women in Christianity."

Niven found herself drawn to a more nature-based spirituality, as expressed in such books as *The Spiral Dance*, by noted Wiccan priestess Starhawk, and *The Mists of Avalon*, Marion Zimmer Bradley's epic retelling of the Arthurian saga from the viewpoint of the Druids and women involved. In Bradley's tale, women occupy a central role in ritualmaking, and the followers of the ancient folk religions of Britain demonstrate a pervasive reverence for the natural world that informs their every thought and deed. "I thought, 'Wouldn't it be nice if someone were doing that today?' " Niven recalls. Someone was, and so today, Anne Newkirk Niven, M. Div., is not a Methodist minister, but a practicing Pagan, part of the "Neopagan" movement that is estimated to have several hundred thousand adherents nationwide.

"What draws people into [the movement] is a love of nature, and an understanding that we're one with nature, not separate from it," says Morning Glory Zell, age forty-seven, who lives about thirty miles inland—as the eagle flies—from Niven. "Unlike other 'new age' religions, we don't look for God *above*. We don't believe in the 'supernatural.' " To Neopagans, she says, it's *all* natural, and "we just don't understand some phenomena.'' Morning Glory's partner, Oberon (*née* Tim) Zell, age fifty-two, is widely credited with co-founding the Neopagan movement—he coined the term in 1968—and nurturing it through its infancy by publishing one of its principal organs, the newsletter *Green Egg*.

In 1961, before there even was a name for the movement, Zell had founded the Church of All Worlds (CAW), taking the name from the religion proclaimed by Martian-Earthian Michael Valentine Smith in the popular science-fiction novel *Stranger in a Strange Land*, by Robert A. Heinlein. Like Smith and his fictional followers, CAW members greet each other with the benediction, ''Thou art God'' or ''Thou art Goddess,'' to acknowledge the ''immanent divinity'' in all beings. CAW remains one of the largest Neopagan subgroups, with some three dozen ''nests'' in major cities and rural retreat properties where seasonal gatherings-of-the-tribes are held. But the movement is nearly as diverse as it is populous: Zell maintains a database that he says includes 800 periodicals and ''a couple of thousand'' different groups. (The small, local Neopagan community of which the Nivens are a part is not affiliated with CAW, but shares many of the same attitudes toward nature, the Divine, and being alive that characterize CAW and other Neopagan groups.)

Mainstream America may tend to think of modern pagans (when it thinks of them at all) as indulgent sybarites with an inordinate fondness for nonhuman life forms—or, worse, as heathens threatening to corrupt the moral fabric of the universe. But to its adherents, the Neopagan lifestyle provides profound spiritual rewards. "What I get out of [being a practicing pagan] is a sense of profound connectedness, and the sacredness of living here and now on the planet," says Anne Niven. "Central to being a Pagan is the idea that you're a Pagan every day of the week, every second that you're breathing. The very fact that you're breathing is sacred."

Joining the Neopagan movement "healed something in me—that sense of aloneness, of separation," she says. "I had felt a great chasm between the Divine and me. I don't feel that chasm anymore." That's because Neopagan spirituality is predicated on the notion of immanence, the presence of the divine in all things. That translates into a pervasively worshipful attitude among adherents, whereby religious observances are not confined to a particular building or day. As Anne says, "The value in Christianity is based on something else: God. In paganism, it's based on where we are now—the elements, the animals, our bodies. It's wonderful to wake up in the morning and feel there's value in what we do now, everyday, not just going to church on Sunday. All of our life is our spiritual practice.''

Niven, her husband Alan, age forty, and their three sons Arthur, age six, Aidan, age four, and Andrew, age three months, do indeed try to carry out their pagan reverence for the world and life in all its forms—not so much in arcane ceremonies as in simple acts of appreciation and mindfulness. ''The fabric of our spirituality is very tightly woven of small details,'' Anne says. ''We don't do large rituals or big prayers every day. It's more like lots and lots of little things, like noticing the weather.'' And so, in the morning, as they leave the house, they say, ''Good morning, Sun.'' At bedtime, it's ''Good night, Moon.'' As they sit down to dinner, they pray: ''Air and water, fire and earth/We thank the Life that gave us birth.'' Anne notes that, with the family growing and their lives becoming more hectic as a consequence, it is hard to do even these small rituals every day—when, for instance, they might not all sit down to eat together. But they try to include such observances whenever they can. ''Rituals are tools. The point is grounding yourself in the planet.'' Even if they don't do the same rituals every day, ''We try to help them ground themselves in living on and respecting the earth, every day in a hundred different ways. It's gotten more informal as we've added children, but it will probably get more formal again once they get a little older. Arthur now wants to get involved on a higher level." One thing for sure, she says: "We haven't gotten any less Pagan."

For the Nivens, as for many other modern pagans, even following such prosaic practices as recycling takes on a ritual aspect, becoming a tangible expression of their spirituality. They eat a "mostly vegetarian" diet, and "try to live our life in as low-impact a way as possible. As pagans, we're trying to be environmental in religious terms. We're environmental because the world is sacred." When they had a mouse in their house, they caught it and released it outside, rather than killing it; when the problem persisted, and they decided they had to kill the mouse, they used a trap, not poison.

Professionally, the Nivens practice their ecopagan values on two fronts: Anne publishes the quarterly *SageWoman: Celebrating the Goddess in Every Woman,* which in little more than a decade has become a leading compendium of evocative poetry, essays, and rituals, usually submitted by their authors, for use by women (individually, in groups, and with their families) to "raise the power" of the Goddess and cultivate an ever-present awareness of the pervasive holiness of the natural world. Anne and Alan are also copublishers of more recently launched quarterly

Green Man: A Magazine for Pagan Men, which "hopes to explore the mysteries of the Gods and Goddesses; to create ritual and myth that celebrate men's connection with each other, with women, and with the natural world; and to foster community between men of all races, classes, and sexual orientations . . . in short, to explore all the challenges and joys of being a pagan man in today's society." The couple also owns and operates Arena Press, a small offset printing company which actively promotes itself as "environmental printers," using soybean inks and doing 85 to 90 percent of its jobs on recycled paper. While the printing company, like the magazines, is no stranger to computers and other modern industrial machines— Anne says some of their friends call them "techno-pagans"—the Nivens are committed to using them in as environmentally responsible a way as possible, and their clients, including several other pagan publications, as well as the local Assembly of God church and secular customers, seem to feel Arena Press is doing just that.

Another important aspect of Neopagan practice is self-devised ritual. Anne put that to good use when she created a "charm to keep us from hitting deer and other creatures" when driving at night on the dark country roads in their area, where many animals are killed by cars almost daily. As she sets out in her car, she imagines a blue light circling her car clockwise three times, and then silently chants, "Three times around, three times about/A world within, a world without." This, she feels, creates a kind of "separation" between her vehicle and any creatures along the way. She adds a silent prayer to Artemis, goddess of the hunt, "to protect the deer and tell them I'm coming. I imagine this as a psychic warning system. And it helps me focus on not wanting to hit the deer and other creatures." What's more, "It works! I have a friend who's hit twelve deer in five years. I've never hit one."

Anne also finds herself at times creating rituals spontaneously, especially now that her kids are getting a little older and asking for them. "My kids are starting to ask me to recite a little ritual at bedtime so they can get the dreams they want," she says bemusedly. "Arthur saw 'The Hunt for Red October,' and now he wants to be a nuclear-sub captain. So the other night he wanted to *dream* about being one, and he said to me, 'C'mon, Mom, can you give me something?' So I made it up on the spot. I did a little prayer to the God/ Goddess. I tried to rhyme it. It was just a few lines: 'Let Arthur have the dreams he needs . . .' "

The Nivens also observe pagan rites with others. When we last spoke, Anne had recently performed a wedding, or, in the old pagan term, "hand-fasting," for two friends. And their local pagan group of about a dozen tries to meet quarterly, at the equinoxes and solstices, for "casting the circle," a loosely-structured ceremony which takes an hour or so and incorporates the basics of pagan worship. (It was easier for them to meet regularly, Anne says, before so many of them started having babies. "When you marry and have kids you don't have a lot of time to stand around and pound drums all night.")

When they do come together to cast the circle, first the group takes time for "acknowledging, saluting, the Four Directions and Four Elements"—Air, Earth, Fire, and Water. Then they invite the Lord and Lady—God and Goddess—into the circle. Next they drum and chant, and dance around the circle, as a means of "raising power, connecting energetically, and *dancing to prayer*"—that is, while prayers are being chanted. Having raised the power, they then release it and rest while sharing a kind of communion—milk, honey, and cookies, perhaps, or red wine and pomegranates: "That's how we live, right? We eat and we drink." Noting the similarity between this sharing of food and drink and the Christian ritual of Communion, for which pagan rites like this may be an antecedent, Niven waxes philosophical: "The spiritual dimension of life has roots in what humans are like, and it grows into many beautiful flowers. I think the Eucharist and what we do grow out of the same need to share as a community." After sharing the ritual repast and talking for a while, the group gives thanks to the elements, and concludes the ceremony by opening the circle.

These gatherings reinforce the group's tribal identity, and, Anne says, create "a magical environment where one did not exist before," in effect "creating a church on the spot. Churches are sacred spaces where people can come together and commune; pagans don't build churches, they make any space a special place. Casting the circle is creating community, a sacred space, and a sacred time."

Of course, you don't have to become a pagan to have a mystical appreciation of nature. About 140 miles almost due east of Pt. Arena lies the Sierra foothill town of Nevada City. A century or more ago, it was a bustling center of mining and trade that developed throughout the surrounding "gold country." In the last several decades, it has become a popular destination for those fleeing the wall-to-wall noise, pollution, and madness of the big cities. One couple who sought such refuge there, Joanne Koury and Steve Reynolds, moved with their two young sons from Berkeley to this town of 3,500 souls in 1988.

Both Joanne and Steve were raised as Christians. Joanne, who worked for nearly two decades as a registered nurse, was raised in the Melchite Catholic faith of her Lebanese-immigrant family in Cleveland; Steve, who also owns a printing business, attended several Protestant churches with his family in Rupert, Idaho— they switched from Methodist to Episcopalian after Steve, then seven, dropped a bag of water from the choir loft onto the minister's head as he entered the church for Sunday service.

Joanne spent sixteen years in Catholic schools, including an all-girls high school and St. Louis University. She received her First Communion in second grade, and, following the Melchite practice, was confirmed when she was baptized (as an infant). She was "very spiritual as a little girl. I got a lot out of ritual in church—a warmth and connectedness to God. My First Communion and that connection to God were very important. I saw God as somebody there to love me and take care of me."

By the time she was in high school, however, she had become disaffected with the church. "I didn't believe what people said; I thought it was very restrictive and guilt-producing. It didn't make me feel good." So, during college, "I just completely said 'the hell with it' and didn't think about it for a while. I always believed in God, I just put [religion] aside."

After college she went to nursing school, and after graduating, she moved to the San Francisco Bay area. When she was twenty-six she became a student at a local "psychic institute," and upon completing the three-year program there taught and gave "psychic readings" for several years. This reawakened her spirituality and reintegrated it into her life, giving her "the physical feeling of connectedness to more than our Earth plane. It gave me an active connection with a Divine Being, whose energy I could feel." Teaching others meant "helping people get in touch with their higher self. That was my goal in doing psychic readings."

Steve, age fifty-one, became an acolyte at the Episcopal church his family attended after the water-bag incident. One morning when he was about fifteen, while performing acolyte service, he looked out over the crowd and suddenly felt alienated. "I knew every single person there, and what they did. Most of those people were hypocrites. They were praying in Church but as far as I was concerned they weren't Christian. I wasn't forgiving or generous with them—the slightly dishonest businessman, the guy who treated his kid very badly." So he became an agnostic, and had no spiritual practice for years, "although once psychedelics came around, that was rather spiritual for me."

Ever since adolescence, Steve has been uneasy with

dogma: "I don't like any organized religion, to tell you the truth. I think they're missing the point. I feel I know the code people should live by. I can't believe in Christian doctrine. I can believe in Christ, but I don't believe what people tell me." Still, he has maintained a personal spirituality and a rigorous moral code. "I considered things spiritually, but on a grander scale, not in terms of Christianity. I saw God as a lot bigger than the world, and not particularly concerned about it. But I still had, and still do have, real strong feelings about honesty and personal responsibility."

At nineteen, Steve went to college in California; in his mid-twenties, his spiritual perspective was further affected when, having been drafted into the Army, he applied for and won conscientious-objector status. "After five years of college and two degrees, I got my nose up out of books, and had to look at the reality of things. The government was telling me to go kill people wholesale, and I didn't think the government had a right to do that." In order to make his case, "I had to look into other religions, and I created my own religion. I picked up pacifist points from various religions, to create a set of principles that I could stand up and argue for in front of people who were trying to break me down." He received his honorable discharge, and says, "You don't go back to being the same person. I was irrevocably changed. I had a really different religious outlook on life. I was much more accepting of various religions, and their good and bad points; I was more open. I was also much more a citizen of the world, rather than the U.S., which increased more as I got older and traveled."

So, having both left Christianity in their early adulthoods, Joanne and Steve had each taken a demanding and typically circuitous path to their respective points on the spiritual landscape, but managed to remain avowedly spiritual through their twenties and thirties. When they married and had their first son, Daniel, now fifteen, they had no particular spiritual "program" to offer him; like so many of their generation, they had to work it out on the fly. In Daniel's early years, Joanne "made a point of *not* talking about God, teaching him prayers, having him baptized. I didn't want him to have that because I thought it was repressive."

It wasn't until it came time to choose a school for Daniel that they faced the need to provide a spiritual framework. Joanne "wanted to protect Daniel from the outside world. I didn't like what was on TV, the toys that were coming out." At the suggestion of a friend, she visited a Waldorf school, whose guiding spirit is the "anthroposophy" of Rudolf Steiner (1861–1925), an Austrian scientist, educator, and philosopher. The first time Joanne entered their kindergarten (which had no kids in it at the time), she cried: "What I saw was a very light, airy classroom that had a softness about it—no harsh teaching materials, soft colors, silk, toys made from wool. It touched a deep part of me, spiritually. I thought, 'Why didn't *I* get to go to a school like this?' It understood a child from a deep level." Consequently, Daniel attended Waldorf schools, in Berkeley and Nevada City, through the eighth grade (he's now in the local public high school); his younger brother Justin, age ten, still does.

And, after moving to the mountains, the family delved more deeply into the anthroposophical view of the world. "The more I got to know Steiner," Joanne told me, "the more I saw he felt you were nurturing the child to become a free adult. I felt I was struggling as an adult to find my own freedom, and saw this as a gift I could give my own kids." That gift, according to Joanne, is given, in the Steinerian view, by validating and nurturing the child's individuality, and by seeing the child with reverence for the divine potential within. "Receive the child in reverence, educate him in love, and let him go in freedom," Joanne quoted Steiner as saying. "Our highest endeavor," he wrote, "must be to develop free human beings who are able of themselves to impart purpose and direction to their lives. The need for imagination, a sense of truth, and a feeling of responsibility—these three forces are the very nerve of education." To which Joanne added, "This is also describing spirituality—when you're developing 'free human beings' with those characteristics, you'll have people who have a strong connection within themselves to the universe."

As Joanne educated herself more deeply about Steiner's philosophy, "the more I learned the more fascinated I became—there wasn't just information about kids, there was information about *life*." Before long, she came to consider herself a "practicing anthroposophist." The dictionary definition states that anthroposophy "maintains that, by virtue of a prescribed method of self-discipline, cognitional experience of the spiritual world can be achieved"; the *Enyclopaedia Britannica* notes that it is "based on the premise that the human intellect has the ability to contact spiritual worlds." A less dry version might say, simply, that anthroposophy studies the divine basis of humankind; the word translates from the Greek as "the wisdom of man." I think of anthroposophy as a kind of admixture of transpersonal psychology and eco-mysticism, but somehow reminiscent of preindustrial Europe: it combines a light-touch Christian aesthetic with ancient agriculture-based practices and

festivals of the type that have long reflected humanity's intimate relationship with nature.

Besides their involvement in the small local Waldorf school, Joanne and Steve became active in a Nevada City anthroposophical study group which calls
itself "Gaia Sophia"—which, in keeping with the Steinerian emphasis on appreciation of the spiritual aspects of the natural world, one could translate as
"Earth Wisdom." Its fifteen or so members and their
partners meet throughout the year for study and discussion of Steiner's philosophy and its implications
for modern life. Not surprisingly, given the importance attached in anthroposophy to observance of the
seasonal rhythms of life, the group each year also or-
ganizes a "festival celebration of the Holy Nights" between Christmas and the feast of the Epiphany,
consisting of thematic evenings spent in different
members' homes. One winter, the evenings included
"Christmas and the Mood of Winter: The Human
Soul's Journey into Darkness" (which a Gaia Sophia
brochure introduced with the questions, "How can
we understand the event of Winter Solstice and the
changes which occur in the natural rhythms of the
Sun, Earth and Stars? And what do these changes
mean for the human soul and its relationship to inner
and outer darkness?"); "The Star Stands Still: Finding the Inner Message of Epiphany" ("Through shar-

ing and ceremony, as well as story-telling and stargazing, we will have an opportunity to encounter the message of Epiphany, which means quite literally, 'the appearance or manifestation of a Spiritual Presence' "); on New Year's Eve, "Love and Its Meaning in the World: Rooted Spirituality and Winged Activism" ("We will hold the last hour of the year and the first minutes of the new year as a time for awareness of the Earth as a living being. Participants are invited to share their special connection with places on the Earth which call for healing and remembrance. A candle-lighting ceremony and prayer circle will follow"); and "Opening to the Angelic Realm: The Real Presence of the Angels in Our Daily Lives" ("What are the roles that the angels play in the seasons and at thresholds such as birth and death?"). This last evening took place in Joanne and Steve's home, and came about, according to Joanne, when, in the midst of her struggling to come up with an idea for an evening, "Two angels came into the room and said, 'Why don't you do an evening about angels?' "

In fact, angels can be found on nearly every wall in the Koury-Reynolds home: in postcards, posters, a calendar, and drawings by the boys. Joanne decorated the house with these images in preparation for the "Angelic Realm" evening, and left them up afterward. As she was gathering and putting up the images,

Justin, who was six at the time, became intensely interested, studying each one copiously and imploring her to explain it in detail. To Joanne, this was palpable evidence that spirituality is alive and well in her children. Another example was a conversation she and Justin had one late-winter night as he was just falling off to sleep, his eyes already closed.

"Mom," he said, "I see an angel."

"You do?" she asked.

"Yeah, and I see God."

"What is it you see?"

"It's too hard to explain . . . God is the King of Heaven, and Gabriel is the prince." Pause. "Aren't they, Mom?"

"Yeah, I guess they are." With that, Justin fell asleep. "Now *that's* a strong sense of spirituality," she said with obvious satisfaction, noting that she had never told Justin anything about the angel Gabriel.

The family took to saying anthroposophical prayers at mealtimes (a favorite: "Blessings on the bloom/Blessings on the fruit/Blessings on the leaf/Blessings on the root") and bedtimes. Notably, the prayers focus on thanksgiving, not supplication. "We haven't brought the kids up to pray *for* things," Steve said. "You give thanks and say blessings."

The Koury-Reynolds clan also integrated the Steinerian program of intimacy with the rhythms and textures of nature into their home, especially after they moved to the Sierra foothills. Surrounded by forested ridges, with an oak-studded hillside falling away from their back door, it became easier for them to feel they were living amid nature, but they learned to make special efforts to bring nature into the home and heart. For example, they took up the custom of maintaining "nature tables" in a prominent spot in the living room, where they could collect stones, plants, feathers, leaves, and anything else that struck their fancy and conveyed the changing of the seasons and other natural processes continually going on around them. The collecting is particularly focused during Advent, the weeks leading up to Christmas; by the time Christmas arrives, according to Joanne, "we have the whole Earth on the table."

This practice illustrates what may be the most important change anthroposophy made in their lives. As Joanne put it: "It's helped me see the importance of living with the seasons, the sameness year after year, the pattern to things, not just in the Earth but in each individual creature. And you see that what's going on in the Earth goes on in our bodies. You feel a connection to God in what you see happening in the Earth, and you see that each of us is a mini-cosmos." After a few years of observing the unique character of each season—for example, the spirit of rebirth in spring, especially in Easter—"I notice I'm living it within me, and it's happening outside in the garden, and in the whole planet."

The sense of "connectedness," which Joanne and Steve derived from their spiritual life, and which grew so much since they began studying anthroposophy in earnest, is not just important to them; for Joanne, it became an indispensable tool humans need in order to face the world—and try to keep the world going. As much as anything, she undertook this spiritual program in order to impart that tool to her sons. "It's so important for kids to grow up with ritual and spirituality," she told me, passion ringing in her voice. "Because of the amount of stress that families live with daily, and because our planet is hanging in the balance. Our kids will have to deal with what's happening to the planet—they're the future leaders. And they're either going to care about the big picture, or they won't. I feel they'll have an easier time of it if they have a good grounding, a good, solid base. That's what the rituals of the seasons, and other rituals, give them."

When she spoke those words, Joanne, despite the great joy and vitality she had found in her spiritual practice, knew only too well about the stresses of daily life and the often overwhelming implications of the "big picture." In 1990, she learned she had breast cancer. She underwent surgery to remove the cancerous lump and enjoyed a too-brief remission, but by the time of our conversations about her family's spiritual life, she suspected that the cancer had returned, and her struggle had entered a new phase that would last two tortuous years. "You know, I had no idea how difficult life would be," she said. "And I don't think I would have made it if I didn't have a strong spiritual base."

That strong spiritual base fortified her effort to rid her body of the dread disease—through chemotherapy, additional surgery, and countless experiments with alternative therapies. Even as the cancer spread and she became progressively weaker physically, her spiritual foundation enabled her to express her tremendous love of life and the people around her. "Our challenge," she wrote in a January 1994 letter to friends, "has been learning to live life fully and in the present, to appreciate each day and to let go of the fear that stops so many of us from experiencing the joys life holds for us. One gift this illness has brought to us is feeling all of your love so deeply." The letter came in a card printed by Steve and designed by Joanne (featuring on the cover a beautifully evocative and Waldorfesque watercolor she had painted); the card's greeting was, "May we each feel the light and love that is deep within us this Holiday

Season, and may it inspire us throughout the year." Clearly, these were the thoughts of a woman who, far from giving in to fear or giving up in the face of an overwhelming and apparently endless struggle, was embracing life, pervaded by a sense of the sacred, nourished by that "connectedness" she held so dear.

Joanne's physical struggle ended a few months later, on May 22, 1994—Whitsunday, the Feast of the Pentecost. She died peacefully, bathed in the love of her family and friends, including one who, sitting beside Joanne as she died, reported a radiance that filled Joanne's visage in the moments after her passing.

The many people who knew and loved Joanne miss her terribly, of course, and mourn the loss of her vibrant presence in their lives, her indomitable spirit, her boundless generosity. But, sitting at her memorial service a few days after her death, I couldn't help but think that, although she had lost her physical battle, she had succeeded in her lifelong struggle to find a spiritual path that nurtured her soul, that offered her a sense of inner aliveness, that brought her, as she put it in her holiday letter, "closer to God." And it seemed clear to me that she deserved, wherever she was, to take great satisfaction in having provided a "strong spiritual base" for her sons, who relish all the Steinerian rituals and creative activities she sought out for them. Reflecting further, I suddenly found prophetic what she had said to me two years earlier: "It's so important to provide that for my kids. I can't prepare them with words for how hard life will be. All I can do is provide them with a strong base, by showing them they have a strong connection with the divine nature of the universe."

CHAPTER 3
Life Can Be Hard

> *God loves us, but kills us anyway.*
> —David James Duncan,
> *The Brothers K*

> *We suffer, yet do not allow the mission of suffering to be*
> *accomplished in us.*
> *I pray the Lord that we may none of us fall into that*
> *torpid state in which our*
> *crosses do us no good.*
> —François Fénelon (1651–1715), French
> Archbishop of Cambray

We often imagine spirituality, or a well-defined spiritual practice, to be a kind of insurance policy, a guarantee of some protection against the travails of this life. One of the most poignant yet entertaining ways I've ever seen this pointed out came at a conference I recently attended. Among the scores of sessions was an "interactive symposium" on death and dying that was *packed*. The next evening, Nina Wise, a San Francisco-based performance artist, appeared at the conference and offered a no-holds-barred send-up of the prevailing sensibility, as epitomized by the popularity of the death-and-dying session, and the chagrin of one attendee who arrives too late to get in to it. "Let me in!'' cried her onstage persona, dismayed to find there was no more space in the room. "I want to practice dying before I die so that when I have to die I won't have to die! Let me in! *I deserve to die!*''

But, alas, enlightenment does not confer immunity from physical death. (Perhaps an enlightened being would say that enlightenment *confers irrelevance upon physical death;* I don't know, not being enlightened myself.) Nor does realization of any given spiritual treasure guarantee that one's life will be trouble-free, whatever its length, or even contented, whatever its attainments. Joanne Koury learned that the hard way. After twenty years of searching and profound spiritual growth, she and her family had found a spiritual path that nurtured them deeply and brought countless blessings into their lives. Nonetheless, she still had to grapple, in her last years, with her understanding of what life was demanding of her, with intense physical suffering, with grave doubts and repeated setbacks and the creeping realization that neither conventional medicine nor a pervasive spirituality would cure her.

We who imagine that spirituality is a kind of inoculation against suffering would do well to consider, however, whether the object of life is to have no problems. The odds are good that it isn't. It seems rather than the object of life is knowing how to deal with—

or at least, knowing how to *figure out* how to deal with—the problems we will surely have. In which case, spirituality is a kind of homeopathic remedy for the soul, accentuating our problems' effect on us by making us more acutely aware of them, but also activating our deepest awareness and bringing it to bear on the task at hand, namely, dealing with our problems.

It's no good, then, pretending that "getting religion" or being "born again" or "finding my guru" will make the rest of your life a bed of roses; the bed may turn out to be made of nails. Canadian singer-songwriter Bruce Cockburn, whose twenty-some albums attest to his highly personalized Christian mysticism, once told me that becoming a Christian did anything but make his life easier. "The essence of salvation," he said, "is freedom—not to give up your choices, but to go where God leads you from moment to moment. Sometimes, that's uncomfortable. You always hear people say, 'I was an alcoholic, then I found Jesus and my life turned around.' That wasn't *my* experience. I became a Christian and I got divorced. It's a mistake to try to limit the spirit with human regulations."

Indeed, the spirit will *not* be limited by human regulations or expectations. Rather, it is because the spirit cannot be limited or directed that we choose and develop a spiritual practice. Whatever form it takes, when we are engaged in it we are *practicing how to live*—especially, how to live with an aspect of ourselves that is not always predictable and may not be completely knowable.

Mark and Anita Weinstein, whom we'll get to know better in Chapter Five, used their spiritual practice, and in particular their unflinching faith in the power of prayer, to deal with a sudden extreme crisis. In the summer of 1994, Anita had a stroke at the tender age of forty-eight. "It was totally unexpected," she said when I spoke with her a year later. "I'd always been in good health—I'd always been the model for everyone else, in terms of diet, exercise, and avoiding bad habits." But there she was, "half paralyzed" from the effects of the cerebral hemorrhage.

Thankfully, she healed remarkably well—and fast. She required less than eight weeks of hospitalization, and today is "ninety-nine per cent recovered." Her speech and ambulatory skills are just fine; she still has some difficulty with writing and other "fine motor skills." But this is in someone who was not expected to recover much of those abilities. "They kept calling me a 'miracle' in the hospital," she says.

Anita and Mark are very clear what they attribute this "miracle" to: prayer. "We really believe that's why I got well so fast," says Anita. "There were people of all faiths praying for me; people on pilgrimages; I was on congregations' prayer schedules.

"Mark was my coach. When I was first hospitalized, I tried to meditate, to do self-healing, but I was too blown out, and felt too much anxiety. Mark came in and prayed with me and for me. He said, 'Thou art That.' He was trying to tell me I was divine, and had the power to heal myself. I didn't believe him. I thought he was in denial. But he kept saying, 'You're gonna walk out of here.' I was weak and couldn't believe it, but I did walk out of the hospital, arm in arm with him."

"Through all this," adds Mark, "there were people, including some close friends—one a doctor— telling me to temper my expectations. It made me angry. I'd tell them, 'You wait, she's gonna walk out of there by the end of the summer.' And she did."

For some people, then, spirituality centers on attending to the wounds and stresses of life: coping with them materially, sorting through their psychological impact and metaphysical import, restoring one's self to something like balance and power so that one can continue living, growing, aspiring, and walking the path toward one's destination.

* * *

In some instances, having a regular spiritual practice allows people to survive, and even thrive, in the wake of a complete rescripting of their lives, including grievous personal and professional loss. It's just as Joanne Koury said: "I had no idea how difficult life would be. And I don't think I would have made it if I didn't have a strong spiritual base."

Nancy and Jim Canestaro found out just how difficult life can be in 1991—when, in the space of one year, they suffered the deaths of her father and another close relative, lost Jim's business and their Blacksburg, Virginia home, and moved to Knoxville, Tennessee, where they both started new jobs, she as a design teacher, he as a facilities planner. And yet the following spring, while preparing their tax return, Nancy noticed that they had had only one doctor bill amid all that turmoil.

Nancy and Jim attribute their ability to handle stress with what seems to be remarkable equanimity to their practice of "Mahikari," which originated in Japan in the late 1950s. Its full Japanese name is *Mahikari no waza,* which is translated in Mahikari literature as "the practice of radiating True Light." The method consists simply of "giving light" to someone for about an hour, the Canestaros say, during which time the "giver" imagines the "True Light of God" coming through him or her to the recipient. In crude terms, one could say that God is on one end of a heavenly telephone line, and the recipient is on the other, with the giver being the line. The purpose of the ritual is to perform a "cleansing" of spiritual—and, adherents believe, physical—toxins which build up at specific points in the receiving person. By performing the ritual regularly, practitioners aim at "awakening through spiritual purification."

Nancy, age forty-seven, says she "stopped following the religion of my childhood nine years ago, when my mother was dying. All of a sudden, there was no one there, nothing to fall back on from my previous Presbyterian upbringing." She had heard about Mahikari from a friend who taught at the same Virginia school where Nancy was then teaching. The friend's brother, a Buddhist monk in Japan, had learned Mahikari there and returned to Virginia to "give light" to their mother, who had been diagnosed with cancer but had not yet started treatment. He gave her light, and the woman's doctors, upon doing confirmatory tests, could no longer find the cancer. Nancy's friend became an enthusiastic practitioner of Mahikari, and Nancy soon noticed that the complaining attitude they shared was being replaced by a bright and cheerful one.

When Nancy's mother became ill, she says, "I had

to have some of this 'Light.' " She learned the method and went to give light to her mother—who didn't want it. Still, "I kept up the practice and found that through it I was becoming stronger and better able to cope with what was happening in our family. I don't seem to be the kind of person who would hold the family together, but that's what I wound up doing." After her mother passed away, Nancy studied the method further, and began giving light to her father, who, to her surprise, was receptive to it.

During the time that her mother was getting progressively weaker through the period after her death, Jim, whom Nancy describes as "very rational and pragmatic," noticed remarkable changes in his wife. "He watched me get stronger, and that impressed him," she says. During this time, in order for Nancy to attend monthly Mahikari "thanksgiving ceremonies," they would drive five hours from Blacksburg to the nearest Mahikari *dojo,* or center, in Washington, D.C., with their young son B. J. in tow; Jim and the boy would sit in the car while Nancy gave and received light in the dojo. She never tried to make Jim become a member. (B. J., now eleven, was too young at the time to learn the method.) Jim eventually decided to join anyway.

"She'd made a lot of progress," he says, "and I hated to see her backslide because she didn't have anyone to practice with. When someone's tormented and they seem to be getting order, and you're not willing to step in and help maintain that order, you're just contributing to the problem. So much of religion is two people trying to seek order"—here Nancy interjects, "and balance"—"together. If you value your marriage, you can either stay with your prejudice and say, 'I don't do this kind of thing,' or you can go with your heart, and say, 'I don't really care what manifestation all this takes, as long as the end result is creating more order in my life.' " When he took up the practice himself, Jim says, he could "sense the order. I [could] sense that I [was] beginning to merge with this person at different levels."

Jim may have been moved to learn Mahikari by the good he saw it doing his wife, but at the time he was going through his own dark night of skull-pounding pressure. He had spent six years struggling to launch a start-up venture, manufacturing software that he had designed. "We had 60,000 production hours into the product," he says wistfully. With a lot of people's livelihoods, and investors' money, at stake, he nearly imploded from the strain, suffering frequent anxiety attacks. He would pray for the success of the business, but as he learned Mahikari and adopted the "faith in God's plan" which Mahikari teachings encourage, he came to realize that the business simply wasn't part of that plan. "I just tried to learn the lessons," he says. "I started opening up and things started happening—including the business failing." Finally, he decided to file for bankruptcy. Although it cost years of his life, and paying off their debts meant losing their home, Nancy and Jim both now see the failure of the business as a kind of gift, a chance to start over. For that, they feel only gratefulness.

Nancy's father had died just before Jim's business had gone under. "The difference between the process with my mother and with my father was like night and day," she says. "It was a very positive time for me—giving as much comfort, love, and light as I could, and totally giving myself to another person whom I love very much. I don't feel he is gone. I feel he gave me a much greater appreciation for what is beautiful and precious in life, and I hope I can continue to grow in the light as I go on and try to share the experience with others."

"I'm a real skeptic," says Jim. "It takes proof for me to appreciate something." He considers that solitary doctor bill from all of 1991. "All this stress, and no physical symptoms. You can say, 'All this is is meditation,' but it's on a higher plane. I focus on the teachings, and they're better at helping me cope than anything else I've run across. And that's what religion is: an institutionalized set of rules to help you cope, and not lose faith in God.''

Nancy adopted the habit of giving light to every room in their home before she left for work in the morning, and to her office upon arrival. (''How can you be negative about your job when you've just tried to improve the spiritual aura of your office?'' asks Jim.) She also gave light to the classrooms in which she was then teaching, and says ''I've expanded the circle of people I want things for. I'm not just teaching my students how to draw; I want them to be better people.'' When we first spoke in 1992, Nancy was preparing her students for a design survey of the cancer ward at a local hospital; without teaching them Mahikari per se, she was trying to infuse their learning of the subtleties of the design process with a sense of how to ''bring light'' to a facility where a battle with darkness is constantly being waged.

''We're not Mother Teresa here,'' notes Jim, ''but given what we've been through, I think we're doing pretty well.'' The ''barometer,'' he says, of how well they're doing, lies in the answer to the questions, ''Are we finding time to give light to each other every day? How often does a couple say, 'For my spiritual well-being, I need your help to focus on the power of God'?'' This couple apparently does it quite often—

up to several times a day. "You've got to find common ground somewhere," says Jim. "You avoid the friction points in your practice. Nancy and I have developed that common ground."

Nancy also gives light to their son, who, she says, loves it and "can't wait" to learn how to give it himself. Unfortunately, the nearest Mahikari center is several hours' drive away, and the family's trips there have become less frequent, so although B. J. is now old enough, by Mahikari standards, to learn the technique, he has not. Given the distance and infrequency of their visits, says Jim, "it's not a sustained religious context for a child." In fact, Jim and Nancy enrolled him in catechism at a local Catholic parish where Jim still regularly attends Mass. "He needs a Christian upbringing because we live in a Christian society," says Jim, who notes that he himself is practicing Mahikari less than Nancy does these days: "I've centered myself inside the Catholic church—for B. J.'s sake. It's important to have a consistent environment for him. So I've spent more time, and Nancy has too, getting more involved with the Church. But there's no disaffection [with Mahikari]." Indeed, Jim credits Mahikari with teaching him the concept of "divine arrangement," in which God's "gift" to us comes in the form of "things laid in our path—tests. All of us struggle with certain dilemmas. The Church stresses that we're all a community of God, that we worship God, but there's less emphasis on the question, 'What is our *interaction* with God?' Mahikari emphasizes that there are these 'arrangements,' and it's up to us to understand them. It's a very useful lesson."

Somehow, B. J., who, according to Jim, "is still interested" in Mahikari and "has picked up a lot through osmosis," manages to bridge the two religious spheres. "He realizes there's not just one particular dogmatic point of view regarding the Godhead/Creator," says Jim. "He knows there are different cultures, and that different peoples speak of that in different ways. It's hard to know what that's going to lead to, but he has integrated a certain Eastern consciousness not emphasized in his Christian background. And he's a very positive individual. He looks for the best in everyone. That's a rather mature concept for a boy his age."

Over the years, he has asked for light when he's been sick or blue, and perplexed his playmates one day when, having fallen and hurt his knee, he repeatedly called out, "Give me light, somebody!" A more dramatic example of the uses of this light came when B. J. had gotten his finger slammed in a car door. "We were sure his finger was broken," says Jim. They rushed to the emergency room, giving the boy light all the way. When they got to the hospital, the

ER was busy, and they waited for over an hour. Finally, B. J. simply said, "Let's go home." They did, to no apparent ill effect such as swelling or discoloration.

Jim and Nancy don't claim that giving light heals broken bones or performs any other kind of medical miracle. But they are very clear that the simple act of envisioning oneself bathed in light brings benefits that are often unpredictable. Sometimes those "benefits" are at first unwelcome, too, such as the failure of Jim's business. But, as Nancy notes, "the Mahikari teachings say, 'Be grateful,'" and what the Canestaros seem to be saying is that being grateful, no matter what the circumstances are, gives one that much more to be grateful for. "I no longer pray asking for things," Nancy says. "I thank God several times a day for all the things that are happening to me, and I apologize for going away from Him or for times when I did not put Him first in my actions. I no longer need to ask for things, as I find that more and more my needs are being met. The more I give to God, the more I find just being handed to me."

A brief personal note about the Canestaros and their practice of giving light. Several years ago, when I first interviewed them, I mentioned my family's saga with our son's illness. They urged me to take him to the Mahikari center nearest me, which was not very far away at all—in San Francisco. I was curious, and intended to do it, but the usual hustle-bustle of life got in the way. But a few days later a most unusual thing happened.

Michelle had taken Gabe, who was eight at the time, for a routine clinic visit, to receive an exam and an injection of medication. It was not a day when we would have expected him to become especially sickened, but clinic visits are stressful under the best of circumstances, and Gabe sometimes required some "time off" afterward to regain his balance. This particular day, Michelle decided to let him stay home from school after the clinic visit was done, to relax. They made lunch and sat in the backyard to enjoy the bright spring day.

Now, Gabe is a great kid, playful and compassionate and very loving, but he is also a full-contact kind of guy, not usually prone to showing his gentleness, except, say, with younger children and pets. His ordeal has forced him to attend to his needs, and he is often without much in the way of "reserves" left over to tending to others. But this day, he pretended to be Michelle's "waiter" and took special delight in "serving" and pleasing her. He brought her lunch on a tray, went back to the house for anything she needed, and just generally acted as if his mission in life was to make others comfortable and happy. When he sat down to eat with Michelle, he commented on how beautiful the day was and how good he felt. "I feel like there's a light shining on me," he told her.

I haven't been able to ascertain this, but ever since, I've suspected that the Canestaros "gave" him "light" that day. Nancy hasn't said it was her, and Jim says it wasn't him, but "that sure sounds like Nancy." I'd almost rather not find out for sure, because I'm so fascinated by the notion that someone could send "light" to a perfect stranger a continent away. If that is indeed possible, what might we be able to do for those around us? What other dimensions of love have been out there all this time, waiting for us to discover them?

CHAPTER 4
A Sense of Self

You can radiate everything you are.
—John Lennon/Paul McCartney,
"Dig a Pony"

For some families, spirituality and cultural identity are fused into one seamless aspect of being: prayers, meals, family customs, neighborhood events, and many of the other rhythms and benchmarks of life manage, somehow, both to express the spiritual yearnings and beliefs of the family and assert its ethnic group's voice into the larger culture. This is especially evident among Native Americans, African-Americans, Asian-Americans, and American Jews; it is harder to discern in the practices of American Christians of European extraction. The neighborhood *festas* and other customs I recall from my Brooklyn boyhood were distinctive enough, but on the other hand, one can be a Catholic regardless of one's ancestry. My ancestors practiced the same faith as Polish-Americans, Irish-Americans, and Hispanic Americans, while immigrants from China, Tibet, Thailand, Vietnam, and Japan would mostly practice different forms of Buddhism.

There are many denominations of Christianity (not to mention Islam) among the faiths embraced by modern African-Americans, but the liturgy of the archetypal "full gospel" congregation, sometimes called "holy rollers," that many American blacks attend manifests the elements of the black experience in this country—including its musical creations, blues and gospel—in a way that the services of the average Catholic church, for example, cannot do for its parishioner, no matter what their ethnic background. But some African-American families and communities are also finding other forms of spirituality to express their unique heritage and help their children formulate a cultural identity as well as a strong spiritual base.

One particularly intriguing example I found of such an effort is located in the Boston district of Roxbury, a ghetto where much of that city's—and this society's—racial divisiveness has played out. There, Angela and Joe Cook direct The Paige Academy, a private school for inner-city children up to twelve

years of age, which grew out of the Black Ghetto Theater Company. in the mid-1970s and which, according
to Academy literature, is "the only private nonsectarian Black institution in New England."

The school offers an interdisciplinary menu of instruction, nutrition, health care, performing arts, and
spirituality expressed in group ritual. Angela and
Joe—they and their colleagues call each other "Sister" and "Brother"—base the school's programs on
the African proverb, "It takes a village to raise a
child." So, in this neighborhood where, as in so many
like it around the country, the element most absent
from daily life is a sense of cohesiveness, of community, the school teaches "*Ngubo Saba,* the seven principles of *Kwanzaa.*"

Paige students begin each day with the "Umoja ritual," sitting in a circle for meditation. At the end of
the meditation, they hold hands and say, "We are
here to live, to learn, to open ourselves to each other
and to the universe, by these seven principles," then
adding a recitation of Nguzo Saba by their Swahili
names and English translations: *Umoja,* unity; *Kujicha-
gulia,* self-determination; *Ujima,* collective work and
responsibility; *Ujamaa,* cooperative economics;
Kuumba, creativity; *Imani,* faith; and *Nia,* purpose.
They then sing the school "theme song," by Malvina

Reynolds: "Love is something that/you give it away . . . /and you end up having more."

One highlight of the school year is Kwanzaa, the African-American holiday observed from December 26 to January 1. The name, says Brother Joe, means "first fruits," and the festival "celebrates harvest, and the hard work and cooperative, sharing spirit of the community that enables it to survive and to carry on from generation to generation, in a collective sense." Its spirit is not dissimilar, he says, to that of Thanksgiving. "It's an attempt to give thanks and to recognize the accomplishments of individuals as well as the community." Almost all cultures, he notes, have traditional, agriculture-based harvest celebrations; Kwanzaa is an attempt to keep that ageless practice alive within the African-American tradition, and use it to express appreciation and nurture community ties. Apparently it works: the school's graduates not only develop pride, self-esteem, and a sense of communal purpose, but, says Brother Joe, "They keep it going. They take care of it. They won't let it get messed up. They reach out and form bonds with the other children in the community, and keep watch over what we have going here. It's like being in the garden. They are their brothers' and sisters' keepers."

Sister Angela and Brother Joe, who have been married for nearly twenty-eight years and have four of their own children ranging in age from six to twenty-three, bring a broad, ecumenical perspective to this work, and to the work of raising their own children. Brother Joe, age forty-eight, was raised in a Methodist family, and is an ordained Episcopalian minister; he preaches monthly at First Unitarian Universalist Church of Roxbury, in nearby John Eliot Square. Sister Angela, age forty-seven, says of her youth that she "was never too attached to any one denomination— I liked them all." She started looking Eastward as a young adult; today, she practices Agnihotra, a Vedic import from India that calls for the burning of a purifying flame each day precisely at sunrise and sunset. Even the names of their children reflect the multicultural influences the couple have known: Ahmed, age twenty-three (Muslim), Israel, age sixteen (Judeo-Christian), Ashé, age twelve (Yoruba), and Paige Crystal Africa Brooks Cook, age six (African-American).

In their family and their school, the Cooks have managed to identify and honor each of the many strains of culture and identity that have made them and their young charges who they are, joyously celebrating the particular wisdom each influence brings to bear upon the individual, the family, and the community. And in the process, they have discovered something transcendent. "The *Ngubo Saba* encompass all religions," Brother Joe says. "It doesn't exclude any. We believe that it's all related. That spirituality is connected with how you think, how you feel, how you garden, how you treat people. Sometimes I say I'm an Episcopalian priest, sometimes I say I'm a Unitarian minister; but overall, we really do try and embrace the oneness of all people, because we all live and share and learn from each other. What has emerged has been a feeling that there is a oneness of all that exists in this creation."

While we have mainly been examining families whose spiritual practices fall somewhat outside the Judeo-Christian mainstream of contemporary America, it is important to remember that even among the baby-boomer generation there are many people who find everlasting comfort and enduring guidance in the living traditions of their ancestors. That's certainly the case with Larry and Dinah Raful, both age forty-five, who have lived in Omaha for seven years with their three daughters, Sarah, age seventeen, Anna, age fourteen, and Leah, age eleven. Both raised in Jewish families, Larry, dean of the law school at Creighton University (a Jesuit school), and Dinah, director of the child development program at the Jewish Community Center, do their best to maintain a devoutly Jewish home.

For the Rafuls, as for most Jews, practicing Judaism is important both in terms of religious belief and cultural identity—doubly so in a city like Omaha, where, Larry and Dinah note, only 6,500 of the 600,000 residents are Jewish, and there are only three Jewish temples (one each of the three modern denominations of Judaism: Orthodox, Conservative, and Reform). Being part of so tiny a minority means having to face ignorance, not to mention outright prejudice. As an example, Larry cites an incident in Leah's first-grade class at the local public elementary school some years ago. All the students in the class were to compose letters to Santa Claus—except Leah, who was given the "opportunity" to write to "Hanukkah Harry." When Larry visited the principal to register his upset at this fabrication, she asked, "And that *bothered* you?" He was eventually able to show how he felt his tradition had been trivialized, but both he and Dinah were nonplused at this assignment, at once patronizing and ignorant.

That ignorance is the more benign face of something that, in its darkest form, changed the course of this century—and, on a smaller scale, was the impetus for Larry's religious training as a boy. His mother, who was born and raised in Hungary, is a concentration-camp survivor. She and her sister were sent from Budapest to the Ravensbruch, Germany, work camp in a cattle car, and she was on her way to the Dachau extermination camp on the day the war ended. She met Larry's father, an Ohio-born soldier, while she was recuperating from tuberculosis in a hospital; they were married after she joined him in the United States in 1947. He remained in the service for many years, and as the family moved from base to base, often living in small towns, they didn't have much chance to take part in a thriving Jewish community. But Larry's mother made sure they observed Jewish customs in the home. "She believed she survived the camps for a reason—to prove that Hitler didn't win," says Larry. In that sense, every *Shabbat* (sabbath) candle she lit on Friday night was further confirmation of that desperate victory.

Dinah's family, like Larry's, was Conservative, but was somewhat less observant than his family. "We were basically High Holy Days Jews," she recalls. "We were observant, and Jewish, but we didn't go to *schule* [synagogue] regularly." She and her sister helped light Shabbat candles, and were confirmed, but did not celebrate *bat mitzvah*—where both Larry and his brother celebrated *bar mitzvahs*. Still, she says, "Definitely, all my life I felt I was Jewish." And she got something else from her family that Larry also got from his: a broadly-felt political liberalism, common to many modern Jewish-American homes, rooted in the Old Testament concepts of The Law and social justice.

Both families discussed the political tumult of the time at the dinner table, and, according to Larry, these discussions were a natural extension of their Judaism. "So many of my friends struggled with the upheaval in the 1960s," he says. "I didn't struggle with it because all those questions—Cambodia, Kent State—were answered in Judaism. Jews tend to be liberal because Judaism is such a life-affirming religion. If I'd have been in a different religion, I'd have been troubled in the '60s. But it was not a contradiction to be an observant Jew and oppose the war in Vietnam, Richard Nixon, Watergate, and so on. Good-versus-evil is a very easy thing for Jews to see. Jews could fight in World War II and yet oppose Vietnam." Dinah agrees. "It's a very moralistic religion, focusing on the teaching of values. Both our homes were very strong on right and wrong," she says, noting that although "my parents weren't very religious, they were liberal." At which point Larry interjects, "I would argue that Dinah's parents came by their liberalism because it's in the tradition."

The couple met at the University of California at San Diego in the late '60s, and in those years didn't practice Judaism much. Larry says that while he was in college "I didn't think much about being Jewish." They did organize a Passover seder for their friends, both Jewish and Gentile, several years in a row, but other than that they mostly concentrated on finishing their education.

They married in their senior year, and after graduation went on to further studies in Colorado, Larry in law school and Dinah in bilingual education, after which they moved to Los Angeles. Although they became more observant after they married, the arrival of their first child seven years later heightened their devotion to their faith, and to inculcating tradition in their home. "You have a real purpose with children," says Dinah. "You want to teach them."

Today, the Rafuls say traditional blessings before dinner, and at bedtime, and on Friday nights the family has a more ritualized dinner, in observance of the sabbath. Following tradition, the girls set the table, sing songs, say prayers over the candles and wine. Before they drink the wine, Sarah and Anna chant the passage from Genesis that explains why the seventh day of the week is special; in this and other respects, Larry says, he and Dinah are more observant even than their parents were.

As a result, the girls, like the generation before them, are developing a strong cultural and spiritual sensibility—what Larry calls "a framework." On the cultural side, says Dinah, "They see our values, and see our life is being Jewish." In spiritual terms, Larry says, "They know they're not gonna start a meal or go to sleep before we say a blessing. [And] I think they're pretty sure there's a God."

And for this family, God is not a divine superhero, but a "Higher Power." Larry says he's trained himself not to "think of God in human form. I think of God as a force. I pray to God, but I don't think it's important to visualize God." Dinah likewise says "I don't see anyone. You turn to strength, not to ask why or blame someone." Indeed, for both Larry and Dinah, humankind's proper relationship to God is not one of dependence, but rather one of appreciation. "We don't see God as a master puppeteer who has us as marionettes," says Larry. "This means both that God is unfathomable, and that we have to take responsibility for our lives. So much of Judaism has been built around waiting for the Messiah. It's also said that 'The Messiah will come the day after he arrives'—meaning, we're going to have to make the world a place where the Messiah will say, '*Now* you've got it.' " Fixing our lives and changing the world, Larry says, is "*our* work."

It's especially important to them, as parents of three girls, not to reinforce the common image of

God as "an old man with a white beard on a throne," as Larry puts it. He says they're troubled by the patriarchal side of Judaism—an ironic aspect of this matrilineal tradition—and is encouraged by a movement within modern Judaism to "include the feminine—what one rabbi referred to as the 'matriarchy and patriarchy of our religion.'" Along these lines, they were taken with a concept taught to them by a friend who is a female rabbi: a mystical sense of the Life Force known by the Hebrew term *Shechina,* which, Larry points out, is a feminine word. But they see less appreciation of the feminine, and less opportunity for women to participate fully in religious practices, than they'd like. "I have a real problem with women's role [in Judaism]," says Dinah. "That's why we're in a Conservative congregation, where the women can participate on the altar."

Notwithstanding their religious devotion and active involvement in the local Jewish community—they live a few minutes from the Jewish Community Center where Dinah works and where the girls attend Hebrew school—the Rafuls also feel a deeper need that is not quite being met by their congregation's programs. They long for a forum that would teach congregants, especially children, how their religion can inform their daily lives and what the ancient stories from the Scriptures tell us about how to act. They want insight and illumination. "There's no spirituality [in the teaching program]," says Dinah. "We want kids who are enthusiastic." Adds Larry: "I would like the Youth Director to say, in the Saturday morning junior congregation, 'We read that Moses came down with the tablets and saw the golden calf, and threw the tablets, killing 1,200 men. Then he went back to God and got a second set of tablets. Now, how does that affect our lives?' There's got to be something in the beauty of the story to reach us. God *forgave* Moses, for example.

"The only reason religion works is that it means something," he continues. "Its just being there isn't enough. Judaism allowed my mom to survive the camps. What spirituality means is that religion matters. If God made us in God's image," he says, taking pains not to use the masculine pronoun, "then we have some divine attributes—and we should use them."

If Larry's mother's imperative—that the family preserve its Jewishness as a continual blow against the darkness of hatred and celebration of their people's survival—was formative for Larry, it is no less so for her granddaughters, and the family continues to find new ways to cherish its heritage more deeply. In the summer of 1994, Sarah was selected to participate in the biennial "March of the Living," the gathering of

5,000 young people, Jewish and Christian, who spend a week in Poland learning firsthand about the concentration camps, and then a week in Israel visiting religious and historical sites. She was one of some 350 American youths who attended after composing an essay and being screened in a personal interview. In Poland, the youth recreate the two-mile "death march" from Auschwitz to Birchenau on *Yom Ha-Shoah,* the anniversary of the Holocaust; in Israel they attend *Yom Ha-Atz,* or Independence Day, festivities. "The kids get to see everything from the lowest point of Jewish existence to the highest point of Jewish existence," says Larry. "There's a little Zionism thrown in there, sure. But it's important to make sure the kids understand." Given their personal connection to the Holocaust, "the trip was even more meaningful for our entire family," Larry says. To top it off, at the conclusion of the two weeks, Sarah flew to Budapest to join Larry and Dinah, who were with Larry's Uncle Gyuszi. A non-Jew who had married into Larry's mother's family, Gyuszi was a kind of Oskar Schindler who "had saved many people, Jewish and non-Jewish," during the Nazi occupation of Hungary. While the Rafuls were visiting, they attended a ceremony at the Budapest Opera House in which Gyuszi received the Medallion of the Righteous Gentile from the Israeli Holocaust Museum and Authority, completing an amazing half-century cycle of courage, perseverance, and faith in one family.

Ultimately, the Rafuls want a feeling of *Ruach,* which Larry describes as a "tremendous, uplifting spirit of Judaism that fills you." And they want to know how to adhere to the admonition of the prophet Micah, whom Larry quotes: "What is required of man? Only to do justice, love mercy, and walk humbly with God."

CHAPTER 5

Seeking the Sacred, Embracing the Mystery

Everybody is wonderin' what and where they all come from
Everybody is worryin' 'bout where they're gonna go
when the whole thing's done
But no one knows for certain, and so it's all the same to me
I think I'll just let the mystery be
—Iris DeMent,
"Let the Mystery Be"

Whether they consciously sought to heed Micah or not, one Jewish couple in Westchester County, New York, have found fulfilling ways to love mercy and walk humbly with God. Anita and Mark Weinstein do this by integrating the Judaism of their youth with the practice of meditation taught by Vedanta, a strain of Hinduism practiced by students and spiritual descendants of Sri Ramakrishna, a greatly revered Indian saint of the nineteenth century. It was Ramakrishna's disciple, Swami Vivekenanda, who first brought Hinduism to the West, giving acclaimed lectures on the subject at the World's Parliament of Religions in Chicago in 1893. Vivekenanda carried forth Ramakrishna's basic teaching of the unity of all religions, and that ecumenical spirit still informs Vedantists, including the Weinsteins, today.

Both Mark, age fifty-two, and Anita, age forty-nine, were raised in observant Jewish homes. Mark says he had a "standard Westchester County Hebrew school upbringing," featuring religious instruction three times weekly, and, "If I wasn't playing basketball on Saturday mornings, I went to *schule*." Growing up, he says, he "felt at home in synagogue," but he "had a more checkered time" practicing Judaism in college and afterward. While he served in the Air Force, he would go only on the Holy Days, "except in basic training, and then *boy* did I go." When he married for the first time at age twenty-four, to a woman whose father was observant, Mark attended synagogue regularly with his father-in-law. And since he entered the service at age nineteen, he has always said a prayer "when I have any meal—blessings over the bread at least."

At the same time, he was "always fascinated" by Eastern religious philosophy, and by "what I ignorantly perceived correctly: that something existed within." The earliest contact he had with that notion—what he now sees as the immanence, or presence in all things, of God—came when he was "a little boy. I remember it very clearly. I couldn't have been more than four years old, and I remember saying to my mother, 'Where is God?' and my mother said, 'He's everywhere.'

"And I said, 'He's in the air?'

"And she said, 'Yes.'

" 'He's all around?'

" 'Yes.'

" 'Then I'm touching him now?'

" 'Well, he's everywhere.'

" 'He's in the closet?'

"And she didn't answer, she just said, 'He's every-where.' At that moment I really realized that God was *everywhere*—and I was moving through God: wherever I went I was in touch with God. I loved that thought. And then I lost that, because I was told, 'He's not in the closet.' It was kind of left hanging. But for some reason, I always looked within.

"When I met Anita, she introduced me to the writings of Swami Vivekenanda, and I suddenly understood very clearly that we were all one, and we were all part of one. And that the Vedantist point of view—that there is one truth; sages call it many names—was really what I believed. And that I loved God, and I cared not at all how anyone chose to worship, and I understood that She loved us too. And that we were all one and we were actually part of God, because we were all created out of the same stuff—there had to be something that started everything. And so that was why Vedanta seemed so clear and right to me, and why it fit. I didn't see it as an antagonistic point of view to Judaism.''

Anita had come to Vedanta after an Orthodox childhood and a thorough rejection of her Jewishness in her twenties. She grew up in a very Jewish neighborhood in northwest Baltimore, and refers to the 1990 Barry Levinson film *Avalon*, set in the same district, as ''my story. There was synagogue after synagogue on certain streets.'' Her immigrant parents— the father from Latvia, the mother Russia—spoke Yiddish (her dad performed in Yiddish theater when he first immigrated), and her mother lit the Shabbat candles. But she began to drift away in her teen years, after having felt unease at a rabbi's fundraising pitch at a High Holy Day service. ''That gave me an excuse to say, 'Later for this,' '' she recalls. ''I began to see hypocrisy.'' By the time she was twenty-two, she had married a Gentile—an Episcopalian from Palm Beach, about as un-Jewish a combination as can be found on this earth—dyed her hair blond, had a nose job, and ''rejected the whole Jewish identity—and the old values.'' During the five-year marriage, she had no spiritual practice.

When the marriage broke up in 1973, and she found herself distraught, Anita turned, like hundreds of thousands of others in that decade, to human potential workshops and Eastern philosophy. At first she took a Silva Mind Control course, as "a gift to myself" to help boost her sense of what she could do. There, she learned how to meditate, and "my mind opened to lots of possibilities—healing, and mysticism." She dropped out of the Silva scene when she caught a cold: "I thought I wasn't supposed to get a cold anymore. So I thought it was a rip-off."

Anita turned next to a wide range of reading materials, most of which she found at the fabled Wiser's bookstore on Eighth Street in Manhattan. She read on Buddhism, *A Course in Miracles,* and meditation, and was inexorably drawn to Vedanta, through the writings of Christopher Isherwood and Swami Prabhavananda. (Isherwood wrote perhaps the most famous biography of Ramakrishna, *Ramakrishna and His Disciples;* the two produced what may be the most highly-regarded translation of the great Hindu holy book, the *Bhagavad-Gita,* or "Song of God.") At the same time, she became a regular listener to "In the Spirit," a weekly program on New York public radio station WBAI-FM hosted by meditation teacher Lex Hixon. Then, in one of those remarkable synchronicities that prompted best-selling author Bernie Siegel, M.D., to suggest that "coincidence is God's way of remaining anonymous," she met Hixon at a conference and took up his invitation to learn how to practice meditation Vedanta-style. "After that all the searching fell away," she says. "I felt I'd found the real thing."

During these years Anita, who is now a school nurse in Manhattan, was working in a substance-abuse program with drug addicts and alcoholics. After five or six years of that work, she recalls, "I'd had enough of that." At which Mark interjects, "Not really. She went out with and then married a recovering addict"— Mark himself. And here is where their Vedanta practice has perhaps made the biggest difference.

Mark had been practicing law and raising as a single parent his two sons, Seth, now twenty-three, and Noah, now twenty. Despite (or perhaps because of) his success as an attorney, he became addicted "to everything but heroin—cocaine, pot, alcohol." Anita helped him get straight, and introduced him to Vedanta. "There's no question in my mind that Anita is a gift to me, from the Holy Mother [the Vedanta term for Sarada Devi, Ramakrishna's wife] or the Master [Ramakrishna himself]." It seems clear that what lit up within Mark was exactly what Anita had found in Vedanta: God, or what she describes as "an inner peace when I choose to let myself experience it; a tremendous comfort, in that there's something to turn to that's real, a force that exists and that I can tap into; and a sense that I'm never alone."

At the same time, as Mark puts it, "As Anita gave Vedanta to me, I gave Judaism back to her." Anita, who had not been *bat mitzvah*, "went to Torah" for the first time in her life the day before they were married. Today she lights the Friday candles, and they go to *schule* on the Holy Days—or, Mark says, "when something good or terrible happens, and I'll go and say 'Thanks!' or 'Help!' " They see no conflict in their practicing both Vedanta and Judaism; in fact, the confluence of the two traditions has been encouraged all along by Lex, their Vedanta teacher, whom Mark describes as a "Russian Orthodox Buddhist Vedantist Sufi." Says Anita: "Lex would always emphasize my being Jewish, that I should be proud of it and practice it. It was almost like permission." In fact, the talk he gave at the conference where she met him "was on 'Reclaiming Your Heritage'—if you're Jewish, be Jewish; if you're Christian, be Christian."

For Mark, it boils down to the questions, "How do I get closer to God? How do I enjoy God? I enjoy God by being all that I am. And what I am is someone who recognizes that I'm praying to God when I'm taking a shower, when I mow the lawn. Any way that I pray is just sweet and fun, and I enjoy it. So I practice my Jewish traditions as I know them, and I enjoy my heritage very much. *And,* I enjoy meditating. I don't in any way find it a conflict. Others might; I know that if someone else were telling me this, I'd chuckle. I'd say, 'Yeah, *right.*' But I know the spiritual experiences that I've had; I know they exist. I'm not some ditzy seeker. I'm not someone who thinks that by saying a mantra, the world will suddenly become fine. What I understand is, I have the right to be aware of all that goes on. And I have to work my way through it.''

"In Vedanta,'' Anita adds, "every man's intrinsic nature is Divine. However great the problems or misery of life may be, they exist only on the surface. I think that philosophy works with Judaism.'' This inspires a recollection in Mark: "there is a way it hooks in, and you just made me think of it. A rabbi once said to me, 'If I were to choose one thing that would be the basis of Judaism'—I was expecting him to say that there was one God—'it would be: Holy holy holy is the Lord; All the world revels in his glory.' There is not one person or one thing, or a tree or a rock that doesn't revel in the glory of the Lord. It doesn't matter how you come to the Lord. If you are a Vedantist, you understand that it's all the same, and we're all part of the same knowledge. There's one God, and you're just sitting and meditating on that one God—which is everything, including yourself." At this, Mark and Anita say together, "That's Jewish." Anita adds, "Somehow, I feel like it works—I don't know if the great Jewish sages would dispute this, but I feel comfortable with it."

Today, they meditate singly and together, mainly at home, occasionally at Hixon's home and teaching center in the Bronx. (Sadly, Lex Hixon passed from this world in 1995, but his teaching work continues to benefit the many people whose lives he touched.) Mark has resumed the practice of law, and Anita has returned to work after recovering from the stroke she suffered in 1994 (see Chapter Three). Recovery, in fact, is a recurrent theme in their lives: for years, Mark served on the board of the nearby Daytop Village sub-stance-abuse treatment center, where Mark and Anita ran weekly family-counseling groups. Owing to her ill-ness and convalescence, they've had to withdraw from that involvement. But Mark's son Seth, who was him-self an addict, also recovered enough to become a counselor. He is now running his own business in Manhattan.

Noah is now attending the University of Delaware, so both young men are away most of the time. But Mark and Anita see the spiritual mark their dual prac-tice has left on Seth and Noah. Although Noah, at least, has on occasion meditated (he told Anita he was "lifted up"), Mark's sons don't practice it regularly—

they're in what Anita calls their "breaking-away time"—but they do understand Mark and Anita's practice "in an irreverent sense," Mark says. "They saw me go from a macho character to someone who understood life was not what it seemed on the surface. They knew I was meditating, and they gave me the quiet to do it." And Mark is confident his sons will come to what they should, when they should. He describes Seth as "like Tevye, sitting on the roof yelling at God. He's not gonna meditate; *he's* gonna tell *God* what has to happen." Noah, he says, is "a very bright, intelligent being, not overly spiritual but gentle." Anita says they and "the boys" have "talked about karma and reincarnation, and those concepts are not foreign to them." Mark notes that his sons "know what this is about. They know Lex; they understand this is a very, very spiritual and God-realized person. They talk about him."

But Mark and Anita practice no Vedanta rituals with Seth and Noah, remaining content to let the boys find their own way. Perhaps they feel that the peace they have found will speak for itself in the boys' minds. "Because I feel it's all divinely guided," Anita says, "I believe they'll be guided to their path." Meanwhile, they *do* practice Jewish rituals with Seth and Noah. "We observe Seders and all the Jewish holy days together," says Mark. "Anita was very aware of the need to get us to do that." When Mark and Anita first got together, the emotional landscape of the household had been devastated by addiction and the breakup of his first marriage. "One of the things I wanted to do in trying to reconstruct the family," says Anita, "was to establish traditions, to have there be certain things we do at certain times of year." Says Mark, "She brought us together to eat again!"

Whether it is the exposure to Vedanta or the renewed contact with their ethnic heritage, Seth and Noah have definitely shown a depth of feeling that might not otherwise have developed in them. As a case in point, Mark cites the words that Noah uttered in the moments after Anita was rushed off in an ambulance, when the shock of her stroke was just beginning to hit him. "He looked at me, and I must have looked like I'd been hit in the face with a brick. And he shook me and said, 'She's God's child. You *know* she's God's child, and she's gonna be all right!' A lot of the strength I needed came not just from within me, but in hearing that from my son."

Life is not all sweetness and light for the Weinsteins. But the spiritual practice Mark and Anita share has forged a bond that has gotten them through their difficult times. Says Anita, with a laugh: "If only we could get Ramakrishna to explain how to stop the shit."

Whatever fortune holds for them, they seem to

have found something no demon or emergency can take away. "I like myself," says Mark, uttering words no addict could honestly offer. "I'm so much happier than I used to be." That happiness, it seems clear, comes from a growing awareness of what they see as the true nature of reality, perhaps best described in these words Mark attributes to the modern Sufi teacher Pir Vilayat: "The human race is very much like water lilies on a pond. We appear to be separate, but if you look underneath, you'll find we're all entwined."

Some seekers find themselves confronted by the Mystery, surrounded by the Sacred, when and where they least expect it; under the circumstances, they may turn, almost despite themselves, to a religious tradition which suddenly reveals its healing essence to them. One such person is Andrew Kimbrell, age forty-four, Executive Director of the Washington, D.C.-based Center for Technology Assessment, and author of *The Human Body Shop*. Kimbrell, who lives with his wife, actress Kaiulani Lee, age forty-five, their daughter, also named Kaiulani, age fifteen, and their son, Nicholas, age eleven, in Arlington, Virginia, grew up a "red-diaper baby" in California and New York. His father died when Andy was very young, and he and his brothers were raised by their mother and her parents in a distinctly areligious home where the major philosophical focus was social reform. "My mother felt religion was the opiate of the people," Kimbrell says. Yet after decades of social activism—a passionate involvement that shows no signs of abating—Kimbrell converted to Catholicism.

Kimbrell says that his childhood pursuit of music gave him "spiritual release," and that even as a youngster, he also could find himself, in C. S. Lewis's phrase, "surprised by joy" when just walking down the street, finding "an extraordinary feeling of harmony, a cosmic sense, a feeling of bliss" that "indicated early on there was something larger at work. I was always searching for why that was, what it meant, but it didn't relate to anything I saw in religion." In fact, following his mother's example, he adopted "the standard left-wing analysis of religion, as 'bad faith'— comfort for your abandonment."

But when the Vietnam War ended, he found himself, like many others who had been active in the movement to oppose it, wondering where that left him. "Nothing [else] had quite the excitement of planning demonstrations, being maced on the Pentagon march, the internecine warfare at SDS—that was your *life*," he says. "I began to realize I also had a sense of spiritual abandonment." Up to this point, Christianity "was still extremely foreign to me. I was not into guilt and suffering—until I began to feel guilty, and suffer. As you get older," he adds with a laugh, "you begin to feel that suffering had *better* be redemptive."

Trying to work through this spiritual crisis, he read Jung, de Chardin, Theodore Roszak, Owen Barfield, and G. K. Chesterton, whose parable of the ship-wrecked sailor, who hacks through an overgrown jungle only to arrive in his own backyard, remains a favorite metaphor of Kimbrell's. Roszak's writings in particular showed him that "the scientific worldview was the problem. I realized we'd been arguing the wrong point. We'd been arguing for ownership of the means of production, and we weren't talking about what the means of production themselves were doing to the human spirit. I don't mean just the machines; I mean the way we do energy, communications, government, law—the whole modern techno-world. Marxists had missed the boat."

Writers such as Barfield helped him see Christ "as a key moment in history," and the "new man created by Christ" as having the "new task of religion"—to "respiritualize" nature and human society. He found himself drawn to Catholicism, because "the Catholic tradition realized a long time ago that life was dance, not chance: that everything has sacramental meaning, that the created carries the uncreated in it, that bread can carry in it the Body of Christ. You may pass a small tree a thousand times, but after one winter when you've had a loss, you see the buds on the tree in the spring, and the tree becomes sacramental, the great dance of spirit incarnating into flesh, with the tree's roots seeking knowledge in the Earth itself.

"The Church taught that in a visceral way, in the eating of the material of the Earth—bread and wine. The simplest child would understand that: God became man, the Son of Man became bread and wine. If that were a fairy tale, everyone would understand what that means about God in nature and God in ourselves. Everyone. It's the simplest fairy tale in the world. And yet for some reason it's forgotten, sometimes even by the Church."

Even though the modern Church may sometimes "forget" it, Kimbrell finds its canon and even its holy buildings imbued with this sense of sacramental experience, what he calls "analogical imagination." He brings his family to St. Matthew's Cathedral in Washington D.C., which has the Canticle of St. Francis—"Brother Sun, Sister Moon . . ."—carved in the walls. "That's the analogical information right there, seeing elements as souls," he says. "It's like no other religion I've ever heard about. The Church teaches sacramentalism as its orthodoxy. The sacraments teach us the great law of analogy. Bread and wine teach us transformation. They're symbols of transformation. They *are* God. People forget what an incredible thing it was that God became man.''

Andy was finally baptized into the church—by "geologian" Thomas Berry, author of *The Dream of the Earth*—after his first child was born. "I felt a new responsibility, and a need to ground my family in a sacred context," he says. As the family grew, they would go to Mass occasionally and say grace at dinner, but had no particular structure—no catechism, no formal religious training. That changed dramatically after Andy's older brother died in the Persian Gulf War.

Kimbrell flew to Germany, where his brother lay comatose in an Army hospital, and quickly became alienated by the questions of whether or not to maintain life support by artificial means. "I thought, 'I'm so sick of this overmechanized, secular culture which has no sense of the sacramental nature of the body, or the spiritual understanding of death,' " he recalls. "I realized we needed to work with the kids and sacred studies immediately."

The children soon entered religious school at St. James Parish in Arlington, which they attend weekly. "They love it," he says. "Their teacher is a real salt-of-the-earth type. They light candles, plant seeds. The stories make sense to them. They enjoy the idea of belonging. And Father Steve does the Children's Mass like Captain Kangaroo." He pauses for a moment, then continues with this sobering thought: "I see the Church as their protector. It's an institution with a great tradition, and learning about that will be of great help to them. It's a terrible thing to imagine your children in need and you won't be there to help them. The Church performs a sacramental parental function."

Kimbrell is not without criticism of the Church, nor has he swallowed its dogma whole. "I have a lot of problems with the Church," he says. "It has abandoned a lot of what it should be. It has become static. It brought the Mother Deity into the Christian religion, with the Assumption of Mary into heaven, [and yet] it has had difficulty allowing women to participate fully. But, it has a monopoly on sacramentalism. The question is, what are we here for, and how do we teach our kids what we're here for? I don't want them to be *Homo consumptus*. I want them to think of themselves sacramentally."

Andy's wife Kaiulani Lee is also devoted to cultivating a sense of the sacramental in her children, but she comes to it directly from her experience of nature, rather than from any doctrine. Besides appearing occasionally in television soap operas and such prime-time series as "Law and Order," the actress had a role in a forthcoming Meryl Streep film, and stars in the PBS drama "A Midwife's Tale." She added a new dimension to her career a few years ago: having "always sought out the natural world as my church and place for prayer," she wrote a one-woman play, "A Sense of Wonder," based on the life and work of pioneering environmentalist Rachel Carson, author of *Silent Spring.* Today, Kaiulani does about twenty road performances of the play per year.

Raised as an Episcopalian, she now follows no particular religious path—"I'm very eclectic; I think the Great Spirit is the same in all religions," she says— but rather pursues a personal vision along the lines of Native American nature rites. "Everything around in the outside, for me, is a symbol of the sacred," she says. "I have no doubt there is a God, a Great Spirit, who created all of this."

In recent years, Kaiulani has tried to develop her awareness of that pervasive sacredness into a more constant element in her daily life, through a kind of walking meditation. "I get tremendous comfort, strength, and calm from the things I see in the natural world. They translate meaning to me in a nonverbal fashion. I literally feel a part of them; that's my congregation. So what I've tried to do is remind myself to take time to watch water when I'm washing dishes, to be with water even if it's in a steel sink, to feel water while I'm in the shower, to watch a crow diving in the woods as I'm walking the kids to school. To let it come to me.

"I believe all the natural world has spirit, but we're so cut off from it. We move through it—over sidewalks, in cars, over asphalt, into buildings—but we've cut ourselves off from the source. So I'm trying to open myself to the source itself. We know that source best, probably, through lovemaking with our spouses, in laughter, in holding and nursing our children; but aside from those very intimate moments, most people are cut off from it.

"With the natural world, there's the possibility to observe it and let it fall into you. I feel changed when I do that. Something comes in and something comes out. It's where I have my deepest connection with the sacred."

So Kaiulani spends as much time as she can find in nature, whether in her organic garden—where the children often join her—or on one of the family's frequent camping or hiking trips. And she finds that her son and daughter have inherited their parents' profound appreciation of the sacrament that is nature. Driving along in the car, she says, "They'll be sitting in the back seat and one will say, 'Isn't it amazing that God created all this?' instead of asking for an ice-cream cone. God is a part of their language." Or at the end of their mealtime prayer, the children will

add, in their own words, personal appreciation of nature's gifts. Young Kaiulani might say, "I thank you
for this great creation, and we're sorry if we've de-
stroyed it; we will work to make it better—please help
us," her mother reports. In the Native American tradition, Nicholas sometimes gives thanks to the animal
who gave its life, "for making us strong."

Other than that, how does this family practice its
spiritual beliefs? "Very casually," Kaiulani says, self-
effacingly, ascribing this fact to their busy schedule.
"Sometimes when we break bread, we'll talk with the
kids about where the grain comes from. Other times
we'll watch birds at the feeder." Although Kaiulani
minimizes the structure in her family's spiritual life,
there is clearly abundant exposure to various forms
of worship and religious teaching. The family attends
Catholic services about twice a month; Kaiulani also
takes the children occasionally to the National Cathedral in Washington, to "keep that [Episcopal] tradition open" to them, so they will hear the hymns and
prayers she grew up with, and "to let them know
there are many Christian views." And in 1992, the
children completed the year of catechism they had
begun, after their uncle's death, in preparation for
their baptism; which took place the day before Easter
that spring.

But this family's spiritual passion apparently knows

no bounds, and respects no denominational borders, for another baptism was also held: an Omaha Indian rite, performed by Father Berry, in which the children were baptized "into the universe." Berry and the family headed into the mountains and there, as native people have done with their newborn children for millennia, the children were "offered" to the four directions and the elements, welcomed into the world, and given a "spirit name." They did this, Kaiulani notes, "not to counteract the Catholic baptism, but to make it larger, to make it cover all faiths. To open it up to a universal praise for the Great Creation."

CHAPTER 6
Teaching Peace

Do not say anything harsh;
what you have said will be said back to you.
Angry talk is painful; retaliation will get you.
—Dhammapada: Sayings of Buddha,
(translated by **Thomas Cleary**)

These days it is easy to feel that all we have accomplished as a civilization is within inches of being thrown away—whether because of arms proliferation, international conflict, institutionalized greed, or garden-variety intolerance. After more than two centuries of constitutional democracy, we find our public discourse constrained and embittered, rather than enlivened and collegial. A few decades' worth of progress on the environment, and on racial and gender equality, stands to be undone by a newly mean-spirited Congress. Our mass-media culture turns on exploitation, rather than on communication. The old American tradition of "Don't Tread on Me" has eaten its tail and become "Screw You"; as a consequence, the tenor of our public interactions is becoming less convivial, our trajectory anticommunitarian. Many people have been deprived of their children, blamed for a modern epidemic, had their livelihoods threatened, and otherwise treated as second-class citizens, because of their sexual orientation. National political figures stand up at their party's convention and declare a "cultural war" on those whose views differ from theirs—essentially, the nonwhite and/or non-Christian. People who don't like their government's policies feel that the reasonable response is blowing up hundreds of people. Thus does hatred become more acceptable.

In such a climate, it is perhaps not surprising, although it is nonetheless shocking, that many who pursue a form of worship outside the mainstream find themselves having to be more than a little vigilant to protect their rights to worship as they see fit. For some, following their own spiritual vision has meant estrangement from their parents or siblings, harassment for their children, or a need to keep a low profile in their communities.

This kind of conflict may be experienced most dramatically by modern pagans: the term itself, to some, means "godless," "savage," "uncivilized"—all terms that have been used to justify extermination of indigenous peoples, religions, and cultures. A woman I spoke with several years ago when I began to investigate the Neopagan subculture, a San Francisco Bay area therapist and herself a Neopagan, said that, because of prejudice, "many people prefer to be extremely private about their involvement. We know of people who have lost their jobs, or lost their children in custody battles. One woman was shot because she had a mole on her chin and the sniper thought that made her a witch."

Anne Niven has not had any particular problems with her Pt. Arena, California, townfolk—she even served a term on the city council without incident—but she has encountered friction with one sister, a born-again Christian, who attended and was upset by the Nivens' "legal but pagan" wedding, and subsequently sent Anne a "long, detailed letter saying I was on the wrong path and should come back to God. She's made so uncomfortable by what I'm doing as she understands it, that we don't bring it up." Otter Zell says that his youngest son, Zachariah, age nineteen—who used to edit the CAW youth newsletter *How About Magic (H.A.M)*—encountered some harassment from what Zell calls "fundamentalist bullies" at the public high school Zachariah attended. "We went to the school and had meetings with the teachers and principals," Zell says. "We said we weren't going to take this, and would file suit" if it wasn't stopped. The school kept surveillance on the bullies, he says, and the problem went away, but it's clear that our society—founded, ironically by members of persecuted religious sects—still has a long way to go before it completely eliminates religious persecution.

Perhaps the most effective way families who encounter prejudice deal with it is by performing a kind of spiritual *aikido,* using an openhearted explanation of their beliefs to deflect the anger and ignorance sometimes directed at them. Zell's mother-in-law is a Pentecostal Christian, and, he says, "being a monotheist, it's hard for her to accept" paganism. "But she knows us, she knows we're good people. And we make it all work, we integrate it all. When we have her over for dinner, we say her prayers too. We don't try to repudiate her faith."

Unfortunately, there's an awful lot of repudiation of other people's faith—even the mere *search* for faith—going on, as I learned when a number of readers responded to my article, "Paths to God," which appeared in the March 1993 issue of *Parenting* magazine. The article, like the present volume, reflected my nonsectarian stance, suggested a gentle, ecumenical approach to talking with kids about God and other spiritual matters, and encouraged parents to elicit children's own ideas rather than force-feeding them one religious view. And I was just heretical enough to suggest that there were, as the title indicated, many paths to God, many ways to have a healthy spiritual life with one's children. This did not sit well with certain readers. "There is only one *path* to God," fumed B. S., from Indianapolis.

She went on to assert "the factual news" that there "most certainly is a perfect way to find God," to say she felt "despair . . . for this man who is so confused right now"—namely, me—and to decry my suggestion that parents encourage their children to find out more about various religions, because "that, simply put, is like saying, 'Encourage your child to dabble in the occult, witchcraft, Taoism, drugs, ritualistic abuse, astrology, or join David Koresh in Waco.' " B. S. concluded by noting charitably that she and her family "have been remembering Phil, his wife, and their children . . . in our prayer time each day. I hope one day they all come to know God, and his only begotten Son, Jesus Christ." Nor was she the only one moved to petition Heaven for Clan Catalfo: "I'll pray for Phil Catalfo and his family that they do 'find' God and once they do, I know God will forgive them for his 'un-spiritual' article," wrote B. M., of Orange Park, Florida.

Now, I will humbly accept anyone's prayers on behalf of my family and myself, knowing that I can never have too many of them. But these letters both saddened and frightened me: saddened me, because it was clear they were so blinded by the glare of their own beliefs that they could not read my words with an open mind, and simply decide whether or not to agree with me; frightened me, because they evinced a need not just to roundly disagree, not even to dismiss, but to *vanquish* me. As though my ideas were not just wrong, but downright dangerous—and not just to the common welfare, but to them personally. What kind of faith, I wondered, is so tenuous that mere words can cause it to lash out reflexively?

For that matter, what causes a believer to become convinced that a sincere nonbeliever—a stranger to her, whom she wouldn't know from Adam—is actually doing his children harm by raising them in the best way he knows how, and that it is her business to intercede with God on their behalf? What makes a devout believer think he has such a stranglehold on The Truth that he is entitled to go around telling others they're wrong and insist they straighten up or risk some kind of Cosmic Detention? Who appointed these people as Hall Monitors of Eternity?

I wish I had a nickel for every time one of my enraged readers took me to task for some error regarding the "truth." Besides B. S.'s comment about "the factual news," there was A. H., of Tempe, Arizona, who, having expressed her "concern," and after taking me to task for several paragraphs for writing "New Age crap," suddenly acknowledged that my "ideas about prayer are *closer to the truth* [emphasis added]." And S. M., of Honolulu, who said, "I believe that if you are going to teach a child something as important as God you should at least *learn the facts* [emphasis added]." I will say this for my critics: I envy them their certainty. In the world I inhabit, it is a lot harder to know that everyone else's religious beliefs are demonstrably incorrect, not just for *me*, but for *them*.

This is not just about a few extremists who happened to put pen to paper. The irate fundamentalists who wrote to the magazine by far outnumbered those who praised the article. Even given that angry people are more likely to write a letter to the editor than are contented readers, we have to conclude that these particular correspondents represent a sizable percentage—far from a majority, but a notable minority—of the magazine's enormous readership, which is to say, of the population in general. Not that this should surprise us: the news is replete with stories about those who are willing to break the law and even commit murder to impose their religious beliefs on the social order.

Why is it so easy to declare another person not just wrong, but so wrong that we can, we *must*, "defeat" them, obliterate their views? Why do the most fanatical antiabortionists feel they can easily justify killing physicians who perform legal, socially sanctioned medical procedures? When did it become acceptable for an internationally renowned author to live in hiding because a politician/cleric declared him an apostate? Can this be what God wants of us? Is this what we want to teach our children about the value and meaning of religion? How can the love of God make it all right to kill someone?

I confess that I have answers to none of these questions. I don't expect ever to answer them, because as far as I can tell, they have no logical answers. Moreover, I confess that, besides sadness and fear, I felt a third emotion when I received the series of condemning letters about my article: anger. Hard, righteous anger; proud, I'll-get-them anger; the same kind of anger that animated my critics.

While I was still receiving these letters, I "offered" to compose a reply, but my editor wisely declined. I tried to interest another publication in an "essay" on the subject, but thankfully, wasn't asked to write one. Now, several years later, I can thank the people who wrote those wrathful letters, for teaching me several important lessons: 1) Without realizing or intending it, I can (and, too often, do) embody the very attitudes and knee-jerk reactiveness I decry in the world around me; 2) If I aim to instill tolerance in my children, I have to be tolerant; 3) If I want to see peace in the world, I have to teach it—and if I'm to teach it, I have to learn it first.

In my conversations with families around the country, surely the most effective instance I encountered of teaching peace in the face of religious intolerance was the case of the Reverend Daito Zenei Thompson, director of the Life Abundance Zen Sanctuary in Kirkland, Washington. One day when his sons, Eldon, then eleven, and Nicholas, then six, came home from the neighborhood playground upset at having been teased and called "devil worshipers," he offered them a civics lesson that he hoped his sons could impress upon their playmates. Sensei ("teacher"), as he is called, was born Eric Thompson, and raised a Protestant in Long Island, New York, and the Seattle area, but had studied and practiced Buddhism in several states and throughout Asia since first encountering it at age fifteen, so he was well-grounded in both cultures when this crisis arose. "The key point I tried to instill in them," says Thompson, age thirty-nine, "is that there are many major religions, and each has its own interpretations and understandings. America is based on religious freedom, *not* Christianity—a point many Christians have failed to learn from their study of American history texts." He also told his sons, "When kids tease you, explain to them that not everyone is a Christian, and it's not fair to make fun of other people's religion." It seemed to work, for, Thompson told me, after that little talk he didn't hear any more about anyone bothering his boys. "On the contrary," he said, "some of their friends are intrigued. They'll come over, and want to see the statues, ask questions, and so on."

Part of what arouses the interest of his sons and their friends is a natural fascination with ritual. "They like lighting incense," he says, "and ringing gongs and bells," at least weekly, at family meditation sessions or in the Zen center services conducted by Thompson. The family consists of Eldon, age fourteen, Nicholas, age nine, and Andrew, age three (Eldon and Nicholas are his sons by his Korean first wife; Andrew's mother is Thompson's Vietnamese wife Tham). Thompson began training the two older boys in Zen Buddhism from the time they were about five, "since they were old enough to ask questions and sit for a few minutes. Kids can't sit still for very long, but it's important to develop a practice to quiet the mind." Now, it's no secret to most parents that "quiet" and "kids" are words that often don't go together, but then most kids don't have a Sensei for a dad. "There are two methods to get kids to sit," Thompson says. "You can be authoritative—'You *will* sit still.' The more effective way is to do it yourself. They'll see Dad sitting and they'll want to emulate him, and come sit next to him."

Thompson notes that his "biggest fear as a Buddhist parent was, I didn't want them to feel weird, because if they did, they'd reject their religion." Evidently, he needn't worry about that for the time being: he sees in his older son, in particular, the positive effects of learning to quiet the mind. "As a parent and Zen teacher, I try to get them to look at things differently. Day by day, it adds up. Eldon is much more calm about things, more clearheaded. A lot of his friends are pretty wild, but he seems to be a lot more observant of things. That's something I've stressed—be more observant." And he's hopeful that in the years ahead, his sons will use the practice even more: "You plant the seed in good ground, and you cultivate it, and you hope that it grows the right way."

Clearly, this parent feels that spiritual "seed" will bear fruit throughout his sons' lives. "Regardless of what your religious tradition is, I think it's real important to have one," he says. "Some of my fondest memories as a child were of going to church with my family, particularly, for example, on Easter, when we'd receive little plants in Sunday school. Later, I felt that, when and if I had kids, it would be important for them to have some religious tradition rather than just a void. As a Buddhist teacher, I've determined that my kids pick up on this Buddhist tradition. We do things as a family in the Buddhist tradition—just as a Christian would do, taking their kids to Sunday school—in the hopes that, when they grow up— whether they decide to stay Buddhist, or become Christian, or whatever—they'll appreciate it. It's not important what they believe, because later, as adults, they'll make up their own minds which way they want to go. But it's important that they do something. Also, having a practice brings the family closer together, rather than everybody doing their own thing. Today, kids have sports, band practice, after-school activities, and Dad has this, and Mom has that; the religious aspect brings the family together.''

Thompson encourages his sons to make use of any opportunities they have to make their beliefs and practices seem less foreign to their peers. When they're asked what their father does for a living, they usually say simply that he's a minister. ''It's assumed that I'm a Christian minister,'' he says, ''but the teachers and school are very good with that.'' He also goes out of his way to demystify his Buddhist identity. "I make it a point to wear my robes [outside the home]," he says. After all, "I have a religious belief that's counter to most Americans'. And yet, I'm a member of the PTA, I'm on the school restructuring committee—I'm just like everyone else, except I'm a Buddhist." For "Religious Appreciation Day," Eldon gave a report on the teachings of the Buddha which went over very well. "The kids in class were very interested in the Four Sufferings, the Four Noble Truths," Thompson says, obviously pleased that his son's simple sharing of Buddhist tenets was so well received.

Somehow, this obscure, American-born Buddhist teacher and father has managed to "teach peace," promote tolerance, and embody religious and cultural diversity in his community and family. He does this not by opposing those around him, but by educating them. "People are ignorant," he says wistfully. "They just don't know. It's important to share everyone's religious faith, so we can find the common threads that unite us."

CHAPTER 7

Notes Along the Path

Oh Life! accept me—make me worthy—teach me.
—Katherine Mansfield

In the many years I have been exploring family spirituality—personally and professionally, in formal interviews and informal conversations, in readings and reflections—I have encountered a host of insights, sayings, and just plain intelligent ideas that have become indispensable components in the spiritual toolkit I use as both a father and a person. Much of what follows comes from other people's ideas, some of it comes from my own. I have distilled it all into a form I find workable, and offer it to you in the hopes that you will too. This grab bag constitutes a selection of pages from one sojourner's notebook.

Ten Tips for Promoting Family Spirituality

Start Early. Before the world manages to get its grubby mitts all over them, introduce your children to the spiritual side of life, as pursued in your family. Every human must eventually confront her or his own spiritual nature, but trust me on this: kids who are unaccustomed to spiritual rituals, conversations, and issues will tend not to dive into them wholeheartedly if they suddenly find you "getting religion" just as they're entering junior high or starting to date. Better to make whatever degree of spirituality you feel comfortable with a regular part of your family's daily life when they're still young.

Important corollary: it's not necessary to have your entire spiritual "program" worked out before your kids get out of diapers. Work it out as you go along, which is what we're all doing anyway.

Tell the Truth. Don't make up what you don't know (or be afraid to say you don't know), don't fudge on what you do know (although you may have to be careful how you say it), and don't spout absolutes just because you think you "ought" to. Do admit your own questions and doubts in addition to professing your firm beliefs, and especially do admit the "truth" (in their own experience) of what your children ask and say they believe.

Do Good. Not to get into Heaven, but just for the sake of it. Do it with your kids. Let them see you doing it, and let yourself see them doing it—not just at holiday time, either. Help someone in need; visit the sick; support a worthy cause; volunteer your time; organize a beach cleanup; be a concerned, engaged citizen. Make your presence felt in the world in a positive way, thereby teaching your kids that doing so is a natural part of life.

Recognize Your Children as Your Teachers. Why else would they have been given to you? In any event, resist the temptation always to make them bend to your will or learn it your way. Get out of the way once in a while and let them show you what's *really* important to be thinking about, doing, learning.

Be Creative. Tell stories. *Make up* stories. Do artsy-craftsy stuff together: make Christmas-tree ornaments, candles, garden embellishments—anything that can be displayed or used in a ritual. Have campfires. Share family reminiscences. Produce your own little plays. Sing songs. Use music, storytelling, craft, finger painting, any any other artform you can think of.

Be Real. Let your emotions be evident to your children. Love them demonstratively, but also let them see your more complicated emotions—doubt, worry, confusion, uncertainty—not to burden them, but to let them learn, over time, that a person is a complex of feelings and aspirations, and that being alive means staying with the process of sorting them out. Also, if they can learn to accept you as you are, they stand a better chance of accepting themselves when they realize that *they* are pretty complex, too.

Remember: The Journey Is the Destination. Don't become so preoccupied with your individual and spiritual goals, or living up to the Commandments or God's word, or adhering to the Eightfold Path, that you forget to notice what's happening *now*, what is required of you today, how you can best serve your family in the present moment. Or that you overlook the blessings and miracles wrapped up in each day.

Enjoy! Spirituality Is *Not* Punishment! Spirituality is serious business, and sometimes a solemn affair. But it is not meant to deprive us of joy. Rather, it is meant to enable us to experience joy—and grief, and all the other zeniths and nadirs of life—more deeply. Also, humor and spirituality are very closely linked; keep your list of sacrosanct Things That Can Never Be Joked About short.

Wear Your Spirituality on Your Sleeve. Not on your chest, like a badge; but on your sleeve, where your heart ought to be—in plain view. Let your children see you being unashamedly spiritual. It won't make you a better person, or even more spiritual, or keep your kids from going astray. But at least it'll get the point across that the spiritual side of who we are is not something to be concealed or ashamed of.

Sing. This one's worth repeating. You can't do too much singing in life. If you have a *really* lousy singing voice, take lessons. But whatever you have to do to make it palatable to those around you, do it. Birds sing; whales sing; people sing. Doesn't matter whether the songs you sing are spiritual or secular. Just sing them. Sing wherever you go; the only places you shouldn't sing are in the middle of the freeway, and underwater. And the only time you shouldn't sing is when everyone else is sleeping.

Make a Joyful Noise

Why is singing so important? To answer that question, I offer the observations of Jill Purce, a British teacher of ancient ritualized vocal techniques (such as "Mongolian overtone chanting") whom I interviewed a few years ago. Purce believes that sound is at the very heart of creation itself—that sound and resonance, in essence, are what we *are*—and that chanting, singing, and resonating, both individually and with others, are indispenable elements to a healthy spiritual and physical life. She pointed out that Western cultures had traditionally built sacred edifices specifically designed to enhance the reverberations of worshipers' song, to produce a kind of "human tuning fork" effect—but that we have largely lost this kind of aural-spiritual commons. Of course, people do still sing together in church, but generally speaking, Western peoples don't sing; singing is something "reserved" for professional entertainers.

"There's never been a culture that didn't chant—until ours," she said. "There's been no other time in history when people did not sing as we do not sing. We not only don't sing anymore, but we don't realize we don't. We've forgotten to do it, and we've forgotten that we've forgotten.

"In all traditional societies," she added, "chanting is the principal way of communing with the Divine and of keeping society in tune with itself. In the Christian world, until fifty or sixty years ago, everyone went to church and sang. They didn't do it because they sang well; it was simply the way to achieve and maintain harmony. By singing, chanting, and intoning together in church, people tuned themselves. Our body is a kind of vibratory system with many different kinds of resonances. If we stop chanting, we no longer keep ourselves in tune.

"At church, people would be surrounded by their family, so they would not only be tuning their own body, soul, and spirit, but would also be tuning with their family. *The family would be in tune with itself* [emphasis added]. And since the family would be surrounded by the people of the village, all the village would be running itself together. All parts of Christendom, to its furthest reaches, would be in resonance with itself by tuning in similar ways at similar times. And this great resonant network would be tuned with the overall Divine purpose."

Nor is chanting and "tuning together" in church the only way in which the role of sound in our lives has deteriorated, according to Purce: "We used to live in a natural world full of natural sounds: the songs of birds, the wind in the trees, oceans, storms—and within it, ourselves, singing and chanting as we praised the Divine. Now we live in a noisy world within which we ourselves are silent. Today, those natural sounds are deafened by the cacophony of city life, car life."

A trip Purce had recently made to New York made her realize how much of our life has been taken over by city noise. "I realized that, if you want to have air, you have to have noise," she said. "You either have to turn the air conditioner on and listen to its mechanical hum, or you have to open the window and hear all the noise of the city, including other people's air conditioners. Just to *breathe*, you have to hear all this noise." And this noise has affected the way we now vocalize and make music. "The only sounds we make today come through the music of the city," she said. "And that's the music of alienation. The music being made today is the scream to be heard over machines. That's our music: alienated screams.

"Until we quiet the sounds of our environment so we can hear ourselves sing, we *won't* sing—and we *have* to sing."

So: sing, already! Sing by yourself; sing with your mate; sing with your children; sing with your congregation. Sing in church, in your car, in the shower, at the bus stop, in your backyard, in the kitchen, walking down the street. Sing with your neighbors, your co-workers, your enemies, and total strangers.

Sing to express your joy. Sing to chase your blues away. Sing to make the world right again. Sing a particularly eloquent song or catchy tune. Sing to someone you love.

Sing because you were given a voice, and that's what it's for. Feel the blessed vibrations coursing through your throat, rumbling in your chest, buzzing in your ribs. Feel the breath of life fill you up and be returned to the world.

Do this, and you will teach your children to know that everyone is a singer, that *they* are singers, that the world is made of song, that the world is made *by* song.

Talking About God

Throughout this book there have been references to God, Goddess, Life Force, and some of the other innumerable ways people refer, whether rhetorically or earnestly, to the Divine. While trying not to conceal my own views, I have mainly left aside the question of how we as parents ''ought'' to broach the subject with our children, preferring to let the language of the people we've met provide us a sampling of the many ways in which this important concept is being handled in contemporary families. It was important, I felt, not to assume too much about belief in God; while the vast majority of Americans believe in God (or "something"), a discussion of spirituality should not depend on an agreement about God, unless it were to be published as a religious tract, which was not my aim. Still, sooner or later the parent apprehending the problem of spiritual childrearing has to confront the issue of talking about God with her children. Whether you believe devoutly in God, are not sure, call the Divine by other name(s), or are convinced there is no Higher Intelligence, what follows is intended to help you introduce the subject to your children.

No parent, whether an avid churchgoer or an avowed atheist, can escape the task of discussing some concept of God with his or her child. The belief in a single all-powerful God is so pervasive in our culture that it simply cannot be ignored. But even those youngsters who spend many hours each month in a house of worship will feel confused if the religious ideas they're exposed to aren't echoed—or at least addressed—at home. Churches and temples can provide an excellent framework from which to build spiritual beliefs, but those tenets will take hold only when parents make them personal and relevant to everyday life. You don't need to have a theology in order to open young minds to the eternal. Just be honest. Don't promulgate a concept or doctrine you don't believe; and don't be afraid to admit you don't know, or to point out that others believe differently.

Exactly *what* you say about God is less important than the fact that you are seeking. "Our kids discover much more from our learning than they'll ever pick up from our teaching," says Polly Berrien Berends, author of *Gently Lead*. "The best things your children will learn about God will be from watching you try to find out for yourself," she writes. "If your children see you seeking, they will seek—the finding part is up to God."

Although there is no one perfect way to find or discuss God, no updated road map that supersedes all previous editions, there are commonsense, universally practical tactics that can help any parent begin to nurture a child's understanding of the ineffable:

Know Thyself. First, it's a good idea to come to terms with your own beliefs about God. Is your deity vengeful? Loving? Indifferent? Is God, in your view, male or female? Anthropomorphic or a spirit? How does your belief enhance your life? Is there, in your mind, such a thing as divine purpose? Or do you simply not know these answers? It's important to engage in this sort of soul-searching *before* you begin the long journey of spiritual education with your children.

Cultivate Trust. From the moment of birth, and the postpartum bond that follows it, trust is a crucial ingredient in a child's healthy development. It is also a basic component of any belief in God (if that's what you hope to engender), for no matter how much evidence we can find of God's work, the fact remains that most of us, anyway, will have to take God's existence as a matter of faith.

In less abstract terms, it is also important to help a child develop, over time, a basic trust in her ability to move through the world, meet challenges, overcome the dangers she may face. She needs this trust both to be able to live a normal life, and to have the capacity to believe in a loving, guiding Force. "No child can find God if he or she feels unsafe in the world," says psychologist David Heller.

Use a Light Touch. By age four or five, many youngsters are already asking about God on their own. But you can always bring up the topic yourself, provided your little one seems interested. A simple observation like, "Sometimes I think rainbows are God's finger paintings—isn't that funny? What do *you* think?'' will enable you to find out if your child has questions or if she even understands the concept of a divine presence.

Be Artful. Use stories and drawings to convey your own concepts and elicit those of your children. Encourage your kids to spend ten to fifteen minutes alone, drawing pictures of God. Just about any rendering on paper may reveal who or what your child wants God to be, and provides you a window into his imagination.

I tried this with my own kids a few years ago and found them startlingly eager to take up the task. Peter, who was then four or five, had a pretty straightforward creation myth in his hands (''Here's God— he doesn't have any feet because he floats in the sky— and here's me: He made me''). My two older kids' drawings had heavy ecological themes. Gabriel, who was about eight, produced a sketch depicting a tearful deity who was displeased with deforestation, while Jessamine, then twelve, drew an angry God, out in space, contemplating a widening hole in the ozone layer. Their three masterworks revealed that, without any special guidance from us, our kids had come to hold intimate, well-defined beliefs about God—and to bear heavy concerns about the state of the world, and what they think God feels about *that*.

Be Playful. Active, creative play can make the search for God "less of a didactic lesson and more of a treasure hunt," as Polly Berends puts it. Try getting down on your hands and knees with your child and her dolls or stuffed animals, and see what she comes up with when you wonder out loud which creature is most like God. Or you can "play God" yourself: stage a make-believe drama and have one of her playthings take on the role of an all-powerful being.

Teach Silence and Stillness. Sometimes the most crucial skill—in many aspects of life, not just the divine "treasure hunt"—is not talking but listening, not going to but waiting for, not seeking the elusive but finding what is there. All of these require patience and the ability to be quiet and still.

Now, I'm not suggesting that you try to turn your youngsters into monks or nuns. Rather, the point here is to develop the ability to become calm amid agitation, to reflect quietly in the face of a perplexing question, to relax and allow inspiration or even an odd guess to come when nothing less will do. Most children can benefit from learning how to quiet themselves—even if they don't find God in the process.

To nurture this skill, Deborah Rozman, author of

the classic *Meditation for Children,* suggests that parents teach kids as young as six what she calls the "freeze-frame game." When your youngsters are already somewhat quiet and relaxed, have them try to slow their mental and physical action. Then offer some gentle suggestions:

"Let's freeze our bodies, minds, and feelings . . . Now imagine all your energy moving into your heart . . . Let's think about someone or something we love— a friend, or a pet, or even yourself—that's where your heart is. . . . Listen to what your heart is trying to tell you. . . . Now speak, slowly, from your heart, whatever you really want to say." If necessary, remind the child to take deep, relaxed, regular breaths.

With enough practice, your child can call upon the ability to engender quietude and inspiration at any time—i.e., when he's agitated or energetic or just posing a question, and the two of you will be able to use it as a tool to help you through a deep or difficult moment. And, in turning to his own "center," the child is visiting the same place where the human heart glimpses God; acquiring this skill can help teach a child that those glimpses are available at any time.

Notice Nature. Most kids have an innate affinity for the natural world. For many parents, the everyday miracles of photosynthesis, birdsongs, cloud formations, and tidepools provide the most inviting forum on the idea of God: children get it readily, are endlessly fascinated by it, and soon learn to appreciate, and be reassured by, the intricate design of the planet, and the intelligence at work in that design. "Cut open an apple," Polly Berends suggested to me once, "and see a star. It's amazing. You know nobody put that star in there, and yet there it is. What child won't have a sense of wonder about that order and beauty, about all this good that comes without our doing it?" (Along similar lines, novelist Ken Kesey once observed, "You can count the seeds in an apple, but you can't count the apples in a seed." Try that one on your youngsters.)

The key is to examine the natural phenomena that are immediate to the child's experience—the season at hand, flora and fauna in your area—because nature, like the experience of God, is not something that happens far away. My kids enjoy the company of their pets, but they reserve their awe for the creepy things in the yard, the furry varmints that occasionally wander through, or the sometimes surprising power of weather. One winter, a series of heavy lightning storms—uncharacteristic for our area—left them wide-eyed and revved-up with the dangerous beauty of the natural world.

Don't Forget to Laugh. We have a sense of humor; could it be that God does too? Well, sure it could. The goofy things that you can find in this world speak volumes about a designer whose usually meticulous sensibility took an off-the-wall turn. Some cases in point: that duck-billed, furry, egg-laying, beaver-tailed mammal known as the platypus. Or the albatross, aka the "gooney bird," which crash-lands on water. Or such monuments to human silliness as pet rocks, hula hoops, or stiletto high heels. Pointing out these foibles in nature and quirks in the human condition can make God, and our relationship with the Divine, seem more lively, more flexible, more . . . *interesting*. After all, if we can't have a sense of humor about God, why did the Creator bestow upon us—alone among all creatures, apparently—the ability to find things funny?

All You Need Is Love. Although it may sound trite to say that "God Is Love" and vice versa, that really is the *sine qua non* of a professed belief in a Higher Power. When children are taught to associate this emotion with an almighty presence, they are more likely to enjoy thinking and talking about God. So mention the connections between love and divine inspiration. Also, show your children how to help an ailing relative, or how to comfort a playmate who has just bruised his knee; let them see how the affection and compassion they demonstrate is readily returned.

Talking about God may be the most subtle challenge we face as parents. Just because you're keen on the idea doesn't mean your kids will be. My own attempts at dinnertime discussions, when I first attempted them a few years ago, often proved fruitless, and after a few days of my reading new books about God to my kids, Peter suddenly declared a moratorium: "I *hate* books about God!" Which only makes sense: I was trying to coax him into it rather than discovering it *with* him.

I suspect that parents and children most readily find God in their life together as a family. Perhaps, in simply grappling with the notion of a Supreme Being, we find each other in new and deeper ways; in the end, the two "treasures" may be one and the same.

Prayer: The Soul's Posture

One of the most interesting things I have discovered is that it is actually possible to pray while leaving unresolved certain basic questions about God or one's belief in a Higher Power. Many of the people I've interviewed seem to feel as I do, that praying is a comforting (and even comfortable) thing to do, even if you're uncertain just who or what you think you're praying *to.* How can that be?

I believe it can be because prayer is not so much about the answers we get from whoever is listening, as it is about our offering the prayers in the first place. If prayer were strictly about results, premonitions of winning lottery tickets and eternal youth would be all that people ever prayed for. No, clearly prayer is about what *we* do or say—and what doing or saying it does to us—as much as or even more than what the Universe does in response. (Besides which, as someone once said, "All prayers are answered, but sometimes the answer is 'No.' ")

Of course, we pray for things, both tangible and abstract, all the time: health or healing, strength, protection, guidance, material assistance, good weather, good fortune, and so on. Sometimes we even get what we ask for. I've prayed for help finding work, housing, insight, and ideas—and gotten them all. Did they come in answer to my prayers? I'll probably never know for sure, but I remember to be grateful for them in the meantime. And that effect on me is precisely what I'm talking about: offering the prayers disciplined me into being humble, then thankful; what better answer to a prayer could you want?

But there is another, deeper purpose to prayer that eventually reveals itself: aligning oneself with the order of things, even—especially—when we cannot see or comprehend that order. The act of praying allows us to relinquish the control over our lives that we normally desire but never really have—that is, absolute control of our destiny, of the forces and fortunes that shape our fate—even while we gain a resolve to embrace what comes next—which is the kind of "control" that *is* granted us, and which eventually leads to a kind of contentment we otherwise wouldn't attain.

The most intense experience, and most profound lesson, I've ever had in prayer came in the fall of 1994, on the day our son Gabriel had to undergo additional tests to determine whether there was any residual evidence of the leukemia for which he'd completed a three-year treatment protocol just six months earlier. In those six months, he had been vigorous and healthy and radiant; our lives had blossomed with gratefulness and opportunity; it seemed for all the world that our dark night of the soul, which had lasted more than three years, was over. Suddenly Michelle and I were plunged into fear and grief, even despair. Bewildered and overwrought, we turned him over to the physicians and went outside to wait. It was a gloriously sunny day, but our hearts were breaking. We sat on a bench and held hands, tears streaming down our cheeks. Somehow I managed to offer this prayer aloud for the two of us:

O Mother and Father of All Things, You whose joy created the Universe, thank you for blessing us with this boy. We place him now in your loving arms.

Guide the surgeons' hands; let them find what they must to make possible his healing.

We ask nothing for ourselves. We will do whatever is required of us, without complaint, in gratitude for the happiness our children have brought us.

We ask only mercy for him. He has suffered so much, and he has so much to give. We beg you, let him live, that he may glorify your Creation.

Amen.

How could a stumbling agnostic come up with something like that? How could a supplicant so rusty find words so focused to articulate his petition? I don't know. I can't tell you where that prayer came from, or where it went to, who heard it or how it was received. I don't even know if it "worked." All I know is, I was grateful to have been able to summon it. And, all else being equal, I'd rather have whatever that was working for me, than not. What's more, saying that prayer changed me. Not in the sense of being thunderstruck by God, like St. Paul on the road to Damascus; I was thunderstruck all right, but it was probably more by desperation than anything else. Rather, it changed me by taking me deeper into my own emotions, my own heart, my own *life,* than I'd ever been before. I learned about the ferocity of my love for my children, at a time when I thought I'd already learned that lesson well. I learned how to find my voice in a moment when I barely had enough hope left to draw breath. I found that, when the fires of your own personal hell theaten to consume you, the mere act of petitioning the Universe offers a kind of salvation.

How was my prayer answered? Of the three diagnostic tests performed, two immediately came back negative, i.e., with no evidence of disease. It took several days to learn the results of the third test, and when we did, we were crushed: it came back positive.

Gabe would have to resume treatment—a two-year program, significantly more difficult than the one he'd completed only months before. There would be some permanent side effects. It would require every bit of strength and perseverance he, and we, could muster.

But I can't say that our pleas were rejected. There was indeed "mercy" in the results. His prognosis was good, because the first two tests were negative, and because the treatment he was to undergo had proven effective. As the second treatment program wore on, he weathered the difficulty and rebounded from each new assault of chemo with astounding vigor; back in remission, he inspired all of us. And we, for our part, have learned—again, in spades—to take nothing for granted, to love our children *right now,* to cherish each day we have together. If any of that resulted from my desperate prayer, I'd have to say the prayer worked.

I'd be lying to you if I said I didn't want more than anything else to pray for it all to have been a false alarm; but something else came out of me instead, and I'm grateful it did. I'd give just about anything if that third test could have come back negative along with the other two. But I didn't get to vote on that, and since I didn't, I had (and have) to come to terms with the reality of what happened. Somehow the words that came out of my mouth that day enabled me to do that.

When we pray, we are connecting intimately with God, or with our inner self, or both. Years ago, I used to see prayer as going to the Big Guy with my hat in my hand; perhaps that's why I developed a kind of aversion to prayer as an adult. Now I see prayer as more a matter of my soul's *posture*—erect but relaxed, alert but receptive, purposeful yet open—than what I say or whether I'm asking or thanking. Above all, prayer is anything that commits my energy to the unfolding of events as it seems God "wants" them to unfold. A kindness to a stranger, planting a garden, a simple act of forgiveness—these are all prayers, are they not? In this sense, anything done with a reverent, humble attitude is indeed a prayer. As vocalist Bobby McFerrin once told me, "I pray and I sing. And sometimes my prayer is my singing."

If you can cultivate in your children the kind of stillness and quietude we were talking about earlier, you will be preparing them to learn how to pray. Encourage in them an openness to the suggestions of their own hearts. If you're puzzled as to where to begin, first cultivate these qualities in yourself.

And pray with your children, whether favorite

prayers from a holy book, or hopeful ruminations improvised on the spot.

A 1990s Blessing Over the Bread

I had the good fortune to witness a sublime expression of personal spirituality about a year ago, when writer Howard Rheingold gave the benediction at a wedding I attended. He said the *Ha-Motzi*, the ancient Hebrew blessing over the bread, which has been recited at mealtimes in Jewish households for thousands of years; and then he offered his own idiomatic translation of it. The blessing, *Barukh attahh Adonai Eloheinu melekh ha-olom ha-motzi lehem min ha-aretz*, is usually translated as, "Blessed are You, Lord our God, King of the Universe, who brings forth bread from the earth."

Before several hundred well-wishers, Howard said the blessing in Hebrew. And then he gave this rendition in English:

"It is an incredible blessing to live on the only planet within a billion miles where oxygen is a gas, water is a liquid, and food grows out of the ground. Whoever is responsible for this, THANK YOU!"

CHAPTER 8
Cairns in the Forest

Out beyond ideas of wrongdoing and rightdoing
there is a field. I'll meet you there.
—Rumi
(translated by John Moyne and Coleman Barks)

Journeys have a way of not going exactly how we planned them. There are detours, for instance: times when the path ahead is blocked or the way impassable, and we must take a route different from the one we'd expected to take, or the one shown on the map in hand. Some journeys go through places where the trail becomes obscure, and the way to our destination is not at all clear; at those times we must concentrate on the details of our surroundings, "reading" the landscape carefully, gauging conditions and choosing a direction that we believe will best take us where we're going. And then there are times when the country through which we're traveling offers so many rewards, such enticing treasures or just plain interesting sidelights, that we tarry longer than we might (or should) have, putting ourselves off schedule or changing the nature of the journey entirely. Sometimes the result is unexpected adventure; other times harrowing difficulty or near disaster; many of us have experienced the unappealing state of being just plain lost. In every instance, the journey continues (even when we're at an impasse); the issue is only, *how* will it continue? Where are we? Where do we go from here? How do we get where we're going? And how do we get back?

Experienced hikers know that when they are traveling through country where the trail may be hard to follow—say, across a granite shelf, or through a dense, infrequently-traveled wood—they can look for landmarks previous hikers have left to mark the way: a pile of stones called a cairn, for instance, or a blaze, or cut, in a tree. Coming upon such markers can be an occasion to bless those who went before us, for they make the way easier to find for us who follow—and, perhaps even more importantly, they make it possible to find the way *home*.

Of course, all this applies to spiritual journeys as well as physical ones. And it has become clear to me, in the time I've been discussing the spiritual journey with families around the country, that these sojourn-ers have benefited from the spiritual cairns left by their precursors. For my part, I have benefited from some they have left for me, and I have felt myself leaving some cairns for my own benefit that I hope will be of use to you. In my experience, they serve to keep us on the trail toward a viable spiritual practice, by pointing again and again to what we're after, reminding us why we're on this journey in the first place, providing a sense that someone has trod this difficult path and made it. And, as I am learning, "the journey is its own reward": I may not know where I'm going until I get there, but until I do, staying engaged in the process of undertaking the journey and noticing where it's taking me is plenty for me to handle, and illuminating in its own right. So it is with individuals, parents, children, and families, if we but see it—and invite our children to see it—that way.

Practicing Together: A Sense of Community

One of the most tangible and valuable benefits people get from having a religious practice is a deep sense of spiritual community—belonging, being supported, doing and learning and struggling alongside others. Several of the people I spoke with pointed out that *religio,* the Latin word which gave us "religion," has its roots in words meaning linking, fastening, or binding together. What we can see, then, in religion at its most experientially meaningful—and least doctrinaire—is that which reconnects us to each other, and to the ineffable.

For Joanne Koury, spiritual belief was "not easy, not something I can do on my own. I need others to help me work on it." Being in the anthroposophical study group she and her husband Steve joined, Gaia Sophia, not only helped further her studies, but also supported her in her struggles: "If I had a spiritual need or crisis, I could call on anyone in that group and get some real help." Taking part in these group activities taught Joanne that "I'm part of the world, part of humanity in a real deep way, more than I felt in traditional religion. Growing up, I felt 'apart from,' different, odd, in the Catholic religion; it didn't really embrace me. Now it feels easy to be embraced. It feels natural. I feel like an insider. And it's easy to see that *everybody* is an insider."

Oberon Zell describes pagan communities as "tribal," and says that this tribal sensibility is "a full-time thing—it's an extension of your daily life." There is within a "tribe" a feeling that "we are a people together," he says, adding that "many tribal peoples' own names for themselves translate simply as 'the people.' There's a feeling of, 'Finally, my own kind.' "

For Larry Raful, whose family is among a minority that makes up barely one percent of its city's population, the tribalism of spiritual community is a powerful attraction. "In my daily life," he says, "there's no difference between me and other people. But in synagogue, there's an important difference between us and others. When I look at the people in my synagogue, I think, 'Their people and my people were together in the Sinai Desert.' We're part of this family and we have this history. Only a few thousand years ago, we were standing in the desert with Moses, during the Exodus. That group continued to hold onto the Ten Commandments, from Sinai on. Those are the people to whom I'm directly related, by blood."

The appeal of this profound sense of belonging speaks for itself. We also know, however, that humans have too often fallen prey to the instinct to demonize those who *don't* belong to their particular tribe. We can take heart in the fact that faith communities are working hard to build bridges across religious lines, to heal the wounds that sectarian divisiveness have rendered in the commonweal. But it remains, one suspects, for humanity to expand that "tribal" sense of "my own kind" to an increasingly larger circle of what Joanne Koury called "insiders"—to create what Joseph Campbell used to say we need: a new, world-encompassing myth of *all* humanity, indeed all life, as one tribe, one family.

While that task remains unfinished, many people who participate actively in their faith communities are deepening and expanding their feeling of interconnectedness with others—through the simple and quite traditional act of helping people in need, of alleviating suffering. Jean Grasso Fitzpatrick, author of *Something More,* says that what you find in churches today are soup kitchens and food pantries—church communities "picking up what the government isn't doing" to address basic human needs—and that this helps the community coalesce around the compassion, "the concept of a loving God," which, she says, is the basis of Western religion.

"I might read the Bible," she says, "or some other devotional text, and say to myself, 'You have a loving God.' And I might go out and walk in the woods and see the beauty of nature and get some sense of connectedness that way, or privately in meditation. But boy, there's nothing like a casserole made by some old lady who pats my children on the head to say to me that somebody else in this world knows that I'm alive, and cares—*for no reason!* It's completely unearned! It's not like I did anything for her. We can try and talk about grace, or love being the pulse of the universe, or whatever, but it's that daily contact with it, feeling what it means to receive, that means so much. If my kids and I bring cans of soup in on Sunday for people who are hungry, and see that we're not alone in doing that, that our whole faith community is involved in the same effort, it makes us feel like we're part of something, part of an ongoing movement of healing that happens in the world. You might describe that as the action of God. Human beings become the face and the hands of God.''

Polly Berrien Berends, a counselor in Hastings-on-Hudson, New York, and author of three books on spirituality and the family, echoes Fitzpatrick. ''You can study Buddhism, Sufism, Taoism, Hinduism,'' she says. ''It touches you, and you recognize it with that inner child-of-God-hood that knows the truth when it sees it. You get a wonderful relief—it's like spotting an oasis in the desert. You think it has *changed* you. But all it's done is make you feel less alone. You can think you know better than the dummies who *schlep* to church, but you may still be fighting at home; you haven't changed just because of what somebody else wrote about. *But,* if you haul yourself off to a spiritual community and you participate there—listen; discern; if you go not just to judge but to participate—you will find yourself faced with a spiritual challenge that is really wonderful. Because, if anything you read in your bedroom is true, it must make you more loving, wise, compassionate, and giving in the human community. One of the most important things I find in spiritual community is the *practice* of what we know. And if what you know hasn't been turned into love, you don't know it.''

Searching for ''Something''

Those who have found a spiritual community they can call "home" can count themselves among the truly blessed. Many of the families I've met are still searching.

These people may find themselves caught between their aversion to dogma and their yearning for community; unable to accept some central tenet of a church that they otherwise find appealing, they remain on the sidelines, watching the procession with longing. "If I could ever believe the dogma, I would be a very happy Catholic," Alexandra Roth, a Falls Church, Virginia, social worker and mother of a three-year-old son, told the *Washington Post*. "I like the stained glass and the bells and the smells, and I love the stories. But it's those little niggling points—like the divinity of Christ—that get in the way. I just don't believe." (Devout Christians may bristle at the notion of calling Christ's divinity a "little niggling point." To those people, I pass along the words of *San Francisco Chronicle* columnist Jon Carroll, who says in his annual Thanksgiving Day column, "I know some of you folks out there have made up your mind about that one, but not me.") In any event, many families are uncertain as to which theological course to set for themselves: Christian, Jewish, Buddhist, Islamic, one of innumerable other faiths, or some nonsectarian form of worship—or whether it is appropriate at all for them to join an extant congregation. (In fact, some families formulate their own, private practice.)

Many can recognize the need for some source of deeper meaning, but can't articulate what they're looking for. Even someone well-established in a faith tradition can have difficulty selecting a particular congregation, even for the same reason that Larry and Dinah Raful found, when they lived in Los Angeles, where there were scores of temples to choose from: "It took us years to find a synagogue where we were comfortable. It was a real struggle. We knew we were looking for something, but we couldn't put our finger on it." Still others find the conditions placed on them by clergy or doctrine too onerous. Jim Metzner, an independent radio producer based in Yorktown Heights, New York, says that when he, having been raised Jewish, and his wife, having been raised Catholic, set out to find a priest or rabbi in an effort to add a spiritual component to the raising of their two young children, "it wasn't easy. They wanted our first-born. You had to promise to raise your kid Catholic—or Jewish—or you couldn't come."

For those who long to join a spiritual community, the search must begin somewhere. In my family's case, when my wife and I found that our need for spiritual belonging was sharper than it had been in years, we began to look for a worship community we might call our own. We were definitely of the "looking for something, but not sure what" school. But we knew a few things about what would feel right:

• We wanted to feel a part of something *old*. A few years ago we had vacationed in England, and visited cathedrals that had stood for an entire millennium. Sitting in their vaulted spaces, you could imagine the tally of voices that had been lifted up in holy song there over the centuries. Their sacred geometries reminded me of Jill Purce's observation that Western cultures had built sacred edifices specifically designed to produce a "human tuning fork" effect. Her comment made terrific sense to someone sitting in a cathedral in Wells, or Salisbury, or Bath.

   Nor was this feeling limited to ancient Christian churches. Between us, we'd managed to visit several important aboriginal New World "power places" like Machu Picchu, Mesa Verde, and Canyon de Chelly—sacred sites that had stirred up an elemental sense of being human. When you gaze upon an astronomical altar used by Incan priests many centuries ago, or upon an Anasazi petroglyph that has watched the sun rise and set for a millennium or two, you realize there is something to be said for plugging in to a continuum of sacred ritual. No house of worship in our region is more than a couple of centuries old, but we wanted to connect to a liturgy that understood the unchanging nature of the human condition.

- At the same time, we wanted to feel congruent with the concerns of the contemporary world. We couldn't accept any teaching that marginalized half the human race—women—by proscribing their participation in the clergy or the liturgy, or dismissing their demands for control of their own bodies. We wouldn't profess any doctrine that justified humankind's "dominion over" the Earth or otherwise failed to promote an overdue reconciliation with nature.

- To be appropriate and meaningful to us, a spiritual practice would have to be resolutely ecumenical. I have learned too much I consider valuable from too many different religions to be able to swear them off at this point. Moreover, I have virtually no tolerance for castigating another's religion as wrong or errant. If joining a church means calling yourselves the Good Guys and everybody else the Bad Guys, then I'd rather remain unaffiliated.

- We wanted to know that the congregation would be thriving and diverse: there should be a healthy mixture of ages, races, length of membership, and social, educational, and recreational programs.

- The rituals themselves had to be uplifting. I have a low threshold for plain or poorly-rendered music, opaque prayers, or homilies based on damnation. I can get guilt and blame and unappealing music any day of the week just by turning on the radio.

- Our kids had to find it worthwhile. In the end, we weren't looking for a place to go as a couple, but rather a place to go as a family. This one was tricky; our kids were not eager to give up Sunday mornings or to take on a new "obligation." But we let this one go for the time being, to concentrate on finding a worship service that spoke to me and my wife.

Over time, first when we were single, then as a couple, and finally with one or more of our kids, we tried the following liturgical experiences on for size. They are all Christian, but that doesn't mean we have settled the issue or reclaimed our Christian heritage. Rather, it means that we began our search on familiar territory. Even after decades away, we know the basic tenets of Christianity, the Gospel stories, and the basic elements of Christian worship. I may not accept Jesus as my Savior, but I understand his parables. Also, visiting a variety of Christian churches enabled us to "comparison shop" at more or less familiar "outlets." In time, as we get clearer on what we're looking for—and not looking for—we can expand our search to revisit some other religions we've encountered before, like Buddhism and Hinduism.

Entries from a Spiritual Shopper's Journal

Our first stop was a Catholic church about six blocks from our home. It's a small parish church, with a lovely, open, domed interior in need of some TLC. We went there on an impulse one day soon after our son first became ill, just to be quiet and try to discharge some of the incredible stress and anxiety mounting in us. We didn't say a word to each other; we just sat in the empty sanctuary for about fifteen minutes. It calmed us, and I'm grateful that the church was there for us. In fact, I've gone back to do the same thing on a few other occasions. We also attended Mass there once when my parents were visiting from out of town. I was dismayed to find the pews almost empty, all the more so because that Mass celebrated the "reconciliation" of about a dozen adults. What should have been, to my mind, a most festive event, was subdued, almost downtrodden. I noticed paint flaking on the ceiling, and an almost total absence of children (despite the parochial school attached to the church). Moreover, the Mass was not only unfamiliar to me—which was not surprising, given how long it had been since I had last attended with any frequency—but it also didn't seem to speak to me. Although I respect the parish for its commitment to the modern "sanctuary" movement and to the large number of local refugees from Latin America, and am grateful that it was open to me when I needed it, I did not feel called to join its congregation.

One recent Christmas, we took the kids up to the Catholic church near the local University of California campus, to see the "pageant" featuring young children in costume who were enacting the story of the Nativity. The service was, of course, packed; our kids had not been as eager to go as we were, and, when we got there, they proclaimed their boredom. I found the spirit among the parishioners warm, but the building itself, with its massive concrete walls reminiscent of the nearby University Art Museum, cold and graceless. We haven't been back.

Next we visited a Unitarian church high on the hill overlooking our town and the entire Bay area. The interior spaces of this church are quite commodious, the view from the vestibule most impressive, the pipe organ dominating the altar a welcome throwback to an older aesthetic in a modern building. The service was multicultural—our daughter especially enjoyed singing the Mexican folk song "De Colores," which she remembered from grade school—but largely formless: there was a long sermon, a few announcements, a number of songs, a moment of silence; but no Communion, no prayers in a customary form. Much was made, as is the Unitarians' wont, of the fact that Unitarian Universalism imposes no dogma on its members, that the church supports absolute "freedom of religious expression" and encourages its members "to develop their own personal theology." (I once joked that Unitarians were a religion "for people who don't believe in God"; my wisecrack was closer to the truth than I realized.) By and by, I got the feeling that I agreed with just about everyone in the room on philosophical matters; if someone had stood up and announced the formation of a political-action committee, I doubtless would have joined. But there seemed to be nothing tending the *soul* in what we saw or heard. Everything seemed aimed at the intellect, and that just wasn't what I came for; at one level, it felt more like a debating society than a church. The irony of insisting, on the one hand, on absolute religious freedom, and forsaking, on the other hand, the one congregation that promises it, is not lost on me. Still, although the people there were most friendly, and the minister called and wrote to let us know we were most welcome—and even though I enjoyed talking with him—we have not returned. No doubt we'll visit again, but not, I think, in hopes of settling there.

Not long after that, we attended a service at a United Church of Christ whose members include a friend of mine. He had made a point of inviting us that week, knowing that there would be a special program of folk and pop songs. I had been intrigued for some time by his involvement in this church, which included early-morning prayer meetings, Sunday school, and serving as a church deacon. The song selection was indeed wonderful, ranging from Hank Williams to Mississippi John Hurt to Reverend Gary Davis to Van Morrison to traditional tunes like "Wayfarin' Stranger" and "Will the Circle Be Unbroken";

they were sung energetically by a four-voice group that included a woman who is one of two ministers at the church. She and her male counterpart conducted the service with genuine passion; their remarks, including her sermon, coming as they did less than a week after the unconscionable bombing in Oklahoma City, were profoundly moving. ("Where was God?" she asked, on behalf of those struggling to accept the enormity of the tragedy. "He was there," she answered, "in the person of the rescue workers. He was there in the face of the fireman, carrying that baby's body to a paramedic. He was in the entire community, which responded so quickly and selflessly to help the trapped and wounded.") I was humbled when the pastor read aloud the intercession request I had hastily written, asking prayers for my son. I knew my friend had kept Gabe and my family present in the weekly prayer meetings, but it was still striking to witness the entire congregation making pleas to God on our behalf. At the conclusion of the service, my friend greeted us cheerfully and with great excitement. Everyone welcomed us; everything had been fine. And yet . . . we didn't feel that "sense of connectedness." Clearly the church members do feel it, and I honor what they share. But we will have to visit again, perhaps a few times, before we can say we've felt it ourselves. I must say, however, that my friend made a comment that has echoed in me ever since. When I asked him about what brought him back to church after years away, and whether it was motivated by wanting to provide a spiritual framework for his young son, he said, with a broad smile, "I thought I was coming back for *him*. I eventually realized I had come back for *me*."

A few weeks later I joined our friend Jane, the mother of our youngest child's two best friends, to visit an Episcopal church near the Berkeley campus. She had been attending there about twice a month for several years. Having been born into a devout Irish-American family, she had, like me, been raised a Catholic; but when she felt drawn back to Mass, she couldn't bring herself to attend a Catholic church, given the Church's doctrines on the ordination of women, contraception, and reproductive rights. Her voice bristles with barely-contained anger when the subject comes up today; suffice it to say she does not speak of the Holy Father with reverence. A few years ago, a friend invited her to this Episcopal church. She liked what she found, and has returned frequently, sometimes alone, sometimes with one or more of her three children. (Her husband joins them on Holy Days such as Easter.) I had always felt kind of funny about the Episcopal church, considering it a kind of watered-down Catholicism sadly bereft of any ethnic

richness. Imagine my surprise, then, to find this particular church's services enlivening, its congregation
variegated, its interior homey and sunlit, its whole feel
inviting. I had a little trouble bouncing back and
forth between the hymnal and the *Book of Common
Prayer,* but that was a minor consideration. I appreciated the fact that the sermon was delivered by a
woman; was comforted by the familiar components of
Offertory and Communion; was thunderstruck by the
excellent choir (which sat, not high above us, but
close behind us) and virtuoso organist; and somehow
felt more comfortable among the several-score unfamiliar faces I saw that day than among the others I'd
seen at other, equally hospitable churches earlier. I
was also grateful to gain a new insight into exactly
what brings our friend back to church so often. "It's
this *other side,* another way of being," she said with
characteristic intensity as she dropped me off at home
afterward. "All the rest of my time is occupied fully
with domestic concerns or professional concerns.
This is a side of me that's not either of those. I really
need to feel that."

Nor was this the only Episcopal church in which
I'd felt privileged to experience something wonderful. I'm not ready to be rebaptized—for that matter,
I still don't think of myself as a Christian—but the
feeling I came away with made me wonder if the most

interesting work being done to reinvigorate contemporary Christianity wasn't being done, at least in my region, by the Episcopal church. I thought back to my many visits over the years to San Francisco's Grace Cathedral, high atop Nob Hill, seat of the Episcopal Diocese. Years ago, our family had attended the first annual "Sing for Your Life" marathon there. Led by singer Bobby McFerrin and members of his vocal ensemble Voicestra, this twenty-four-hour formless chant had entirely captivated us (even the kids, who were ages eleven, seven and four at the time) and shown how a structure that had been passed down through the centuries—the Gothic cathedral—could be used to minister to contemporary spiritual needs.

In the midst of our tour of local churches, I returned to Grace one late-winter Friday evening, to experience a "Taize" (pronounced "tie-zay") ceremony. Taize combines chant, prayer, music, and a kind of group spiritual calisthenic. According to a flyer I picked up, the service originated in Taize, France, "in an interfaith community of eighty brothers from twenty countries," and "is dedicated to the reconciliation of all Christians and to intercession and work on behalf of the poor." Taize is gaining in popularity at churches around the U.S., and apparently varies greatly from church to church, but is mainly based on a series of short, simple chants composed by one Jacques Berthier, "organist at St. Ignatius, Paris, and a friend of Taize." The ceremony I attended at Grace was further enriched by the opportunity to "walk the Labyrinth" while hearing or saying the chants. The Labyrinth is a replica of the design laid in the floor of the Chartres Cathedral in the early thirteenth Century; there is only one path in, leading to the sacred center. Walking the labyrinth at any time is a particular kind of meditation; doing it during Taize proved to be wonderfully restorative, healing, and comforting. I would have been happy for it to go on all through the night.

But Taize, wonderful as it was, had nothing on the Planetary Mass.

Glory Be to Gaia

The first thing I noticed when I entered the room were the video screens. There were about a dozen of them, in various sizes, the most striking of which was a large white globe hanging from the ceiling in the middle of the room, serving as a spherical projection surface. Directly below the globe stood an unusual circular table that looked at once like a neolithic artifact and a prop from the set of *Star Trek*. Atop the table, underneath a Plexiglas pyramid, was a crystal chalice. Off to one side was an impressive bank of audio and video consoles and a production crew to run them. As the crowd filed in—many of them recruited from the twentysomething "club scene" and from local environmental groups—the sound system played soothing space music, and the video monitors showed footage of cloudlike patterns. Occasional laser lights flickered. The music gradually segued into a light hip-hop, then escalated into a more arresting dance beat.

No, this wasn't a late-night "rave" party. It was the start of a "Planetary Mass," a form of multimedia worship spawned nearly a decade ago in Sheffield, England, by a passionate young band of Anglicans called the Nine O'Clock Service (NOS) community. At the invitation of William Swing, Episcopal Bishop of California, some thirty-five NOS members had come to San Francisco to stage their Mass at Grace Cathedral twice over the course of this October weekend.

The ritual, also known as the "rave Mass," was inspired by the work of maverick priest Matthew Fox, as well as by the "new creation story" propounded by the likes of theologian Thomas Berry and cosmologist Brian Swimme. The NOS group, comprising some 300 musicians, artists, activists, and others, have adopted the festive techno-pop sensibilities of the "club culture" to devise a spiritual ritual that reflects their concerns for the planet and their hopes for its future.

Waiting for the Mass to begin, I reflected back on my religious career. When I stopped going to church a quarter-century earlier, it was because, like so many other baby boomers, I had chafed under the aegis of restrictive church dogma. But, more importantly, what the Church offered me simply did not meet my spiritual needs. I'm not talking about just the words and rituals performed at services, but about the cosmology contained in Church teachings—the fundamental beliefs about humankind and the world we inhabit. So, like many of my peers, I dropped out, later to dabble in Eastern religions and other forms of mystical experience. Yet I often found myself wondering whether, if my social conscience and spiritual curiosity had been nurtured by the Church, I might still feel at home within it.

Which was why I was so intrigued to discover the "creation spirituality" of Matthew Fox, whose book *Original Blessing*, in its very title, countered what, in large part, had driven me away from the Church. Fox's writings reclaimed the Christian spiritual heritage of mystics such as Meister Eckhart and Hildegard of Bingen; a heritage that did not subjugate the feminine, that did not construe faith and joy as polar opposites. In contrast, argued Fox, institutionalized Christianity, along with the industrialized civilization that grew up around it, is an aberration, a life-threatening wrong turn.

Well, I was not going to differ with that point. But where, I wondered, was this life-affirming religion? Where is there a form of Christian worship that transcends consumer culture, reactionary politics, and contemporary cynicism? Well, as it turns out: in the Planetary Mass.

As the brisk air of harvesttime portended the coming winter, I found myself among some 300 curious people arriving at Grace Cathedral. It seemed fitting that the country's first Planetary Mass should be held there, a site familiar to me as the setting of more than a few epiphanies and welcome experiments in spirituality. The services were being held not in the cathedral's great nave, but in one of its basement rooms, better suited to creating a plugged-in, interactive, postmodern crypt.

After the congregants were settled, a group of a half a dozen men and women circled the round altar carrying votive flames, then positioned themselves around the room. A voice, hard to locate at first, told us that we could, if we liked, move toward one of the flame bearers to pray, and that this was done to "invoke Spirit." As a few people did this, a woman in a white robe ambled about chanting into a wireless-microphone. She was Lori Camm, one of three celebrants; the other two were similarly robed and wireless-miked: Matthew Wright—who accompanied Camm's chant on flute—and Chris Brain. Brain, the first (and so far only) member of the NOS community to be ordained an Anglican priest, also wore, around his neck, a stole and a pendant in the shape of the sun.

Now Camm's image appeared on the monitors and on the white hanging globe. She welcomed us, and thanked San Francisco for welcoming them. After Wright and Brain made brief comments, Camm pointed out the altar's circular shape, noting that it symbolized the fact that "we're all equal." She went on to quote a favored NOS aphorism, which expresses the group's participatory ideal: "the posse is the priest." Then she concluded, near-rapturously, by saying that "the whole universe is grace."

There followed a quick, video-prompted call-and-response ("Eternal justice/*Her presence is with us*"). An energetic male-female singing duo—suddenly illuminated near the altar—led a throbbing dance-beat chant. As we danced, already exulting, we sang along, reading from the monitors:

Now we feel your Life-force rising!
Raise the Passion ten times ten!
Now we breathe you, Christ, inside us,
Feel the freedom pushing on!
Feel the freedom!
Feel the freedom!
Feel the freedom!
Feel the freedom!

When the chant concluded, Wright led us in a series of physical, vocal, and mental meditations. First,
a *T'ai Chi*–like calisthenic: standing, raising our hands
slowly upward and downward, we were urged to
"breathe in—life; breathe out—fear; breathe in—
passion; breathe out—despair; breathe in—hope;
breathe out—death." Next, we sat and simply
breathed, in contemplation of the "oneness of all humanity in the love of God." From this we moved into
a chant of the ancient Aramaic word *Abba* ("Father").

With the congregation thus attuned, Brain sol-
emnly read a quote from Lester Brown of the
Worldwatch Institute, a Washington, D.C.–based environmental think tank, that spoke to the urgent need
for cultural change in light of our advanced state of
ecological deterioration. He concisely translated
Brown's remark into theological terms: " 'The King-
dom of God' is not synonymous with the Church.

It's synonymous with *all of life*—and that means one thing: We *all* are saved, or we all must die.''

Clearly, Brain added, in light of "our cynicism, our sexism, our consumerism," it's incumbent upon us to "do some letting go. So let's do some of that now: confessing our sins to God." What followed was the most supercharged video portion of the Mass, offering a steady barrage of words—"factions . . . adultery . . . sorcery" (this last intercut with footage of a televangelist)—and images that neatly summed up the vanities, paradoxes, and blind spots of the modern world: scenes of Judas Iscariot betraying Christ with a kiss (from the film *The Last Temptation of Christ*) juxtaposed with Bill Clinton and John Major, starving Third World children, high-tech warfare. These yielded to a litany of "virtues" with which we might replace the "sins": "Vicious Love . . . Aggressive Patience . . . Furious Generosity . . . Passionate Faithfulness . . . Ecstatic Gentleness"; interspersed with time-lapse nature footage and accented by a young man doing a hip-hop dance in a spotlight before the altar.

A quick recitation of the *Kyrie* ("Lord, have mercy/ Christ, have mercy/Lord, have mercy") led to a Gospel reading, from the opening verses of John: "In the beginning was the Word . . ." When this was finished, the celebrants and the congregation exchanged what was, to my mind, the most sublime dialogue in the entire service: "This is the Gospel of Christ/*Thank you, Eternal Voice.*"

From among the worshipers seated on the floor, Matthew Fox himself arose to deliver the sermon. "Where is the promise?" Fox began, referring to the promise of eternal salvation inherent in the Word. His answer: "The Light of the Divine One is in each of us." Our reductionist society, Fox explained, has "lassoed" this Light and made it serve military, industrial, entertainment, and business purposes, causing us to lose sight of "what a gift it is just to be alive, to be well, to be together on this planet."

Indeed, Fox went on, "Our species got so excited about texts"—information and scientific knowledge— "that we associated 'the Word of God' with books, and we forgot something ancient: that, as Meister Eckhart said, Every creature is a word of God." With the advent of the printing press, he continued, "we anthropocentrized the Word. But 'In the *beginning* was the Word'—that's fourteen billion years ago! The Word of God is everywhere . . . What we've longed for . . . is a language to express our mysticism. Perhaps now, in the postmodern age, it's emerging: the language of Light."

Fox recalled his first encounter, a year earlier, with the NOS community, "the people here teaching us to pray in a new way—and in a very ancient way: with more dancing, and fewer books." He cited an observation by West African medicine man and cross-cultural workshop leader Malidoma Somé, to the effect that "when a culture loses its spirituality, only the young can bring it back." He noted that the young people of the NOS community—average age twenty-seven—seem to have embarked on just such an endeavor. "The task of bringing it back is so great that it takes a lifetime commitment," Fox said. But "I'm convinced that young people around the world are ready for this kind of strength and commitment so evident" in the NOS community. Also, he continued, "we older people are hungry, we are thirsty—we're ready to learn. That Light burns so brightly in all of us that darkness shall not overcome it."

Fox's words yielded to the festive *Sanctus* chant (celebrating billions of years of "cosmic evolution"), which led into the Communion, the part of the Mass that convinced me that I was witnessing something truly innovative and valuable. Half a dozen people circled the altar, each carrying a sacramental substance. One carried wafers, another wine; but there were also earth, air, fire, and water (I understood this as a Communion of the Elements). As each substance was offered, a brief benediction was uttered—for example, "Christ our Liberator/In our global village we offer bread/In the presence of those who starve." When the earth that sustains us was also presented, Brain said, "I wash my hands in this soil," mixed his fingers in the dark loam, and then wiped them off on his vestments.

Soon the familiar wafers and wine of the Eucharist were taken to different points around the altar, where any who wished could come to receive Communion. In various spots around the room several men and women twirled, in proper dervish stance, while Camm sang "The First Time Ever I Saw Your Face." As I watched a few communicants receive the sacrament I wondered, how long has it been ... twenty years? I couldn't remember when I'd last received Communion. Suddenly this seemed like a perfect time to break the fast.

I stepped up to a woman holding a chalice full of consecrated wafers. She took one, dipped it into a chalice of consecrated wine, and offered it to me with the admonition, "Body of Christ." How many hundreds, even thousands, of times, had I heard that phrase, yet never fully appreciated it. But for one moment I was able to see that, by taking Communion, I was partaking of the life force that fuels Creation; able to perceive of myself as a part of the divine Body of the universe receiving the energy of the "cosmic Christ." As the wafer slid down my throat, it felt surprisingly substantial, and the wine ignited a wonderful warmth.

I enjoyed it so much, in fact, that I went back for seconds a few minutes later. I wasn't sure this was kosher, so I asked if I could take Communion again "for someone who isn't here." I wanted to invoke this loving energy on behalf of my son, who had, only a few weeks earlier, begun the new, more arduous treatment program. I was asked to give his name. "Gabriel, 'Messenger of God,'" I answered.

Again, I received the Eucharist, and I felt that welcome warmth. As I sat down I concentrated on quieting my mind and seeing my family in the loving heart of all Creation. It was not hard to do.

I could do this again, I thought.

After the Communion, things drew rapidly to a close. The celebrants exhorted us to "release the leadership, vision, and creativity in your people," as a way of charging us with continuing the sacred work of reinspiriting our culture. "Lord, in your mercy . . ." they pleaded; "Hear our prayer," we answered. A joyous, lengthy, boogie-down dance ensued, with everyone up and churning their vital juices. It could scarcely have been more primal had we built a bonfire in the middle of the room. When it was over, the celebrants proclaimed, "The Mass is over, go in peace." Came our reply: "*Thank you, Eternal God.*"

*   *   *

One of the more remarkable aspects of this service is that it has developed, and continues to unfold, under the sponsorship of a mainstream Christian denomination. At a postservice press conference, Brain, Camm, and Wright talked about their relationship with the Church of England. After a tenuous start a decade or more ago, they now enjoy great interest and encouragement from their mother church. Many clergy from Sheffield and elsewhere, including archdeacons, visit their services, said Wright, and other Christian communities around England have been inspired to craft similar "postmodern" rituals of their own.

Apparently the Anglican hierarchy embraces this trend not only as a cool way to attract the media-bred younger generation back into the church, but also as a natural expression of contemporary spirituality and an appropriate response to humanity's predicament. At this same press conference, Bishop Swing—who was seen shaking his holiness during the service—also spoke. "We're coming to a moment in history where we've got to fish or cut bait with regard to Nature," Swing observed. "Did Jesus die for all people, or for all Creation *including* people? The Mass we saw tonight was like John the Baptist—a forerunner. I was very excited by tonight."

During my lifetime, I've seen seismic upheavals in the Catholic church, the faith into which I was born, as well as great shifts in its trajectory: Vatican II and the openness of Pope John XXIII's reign, followed by the doctrinaire regressiveness of Paul VI and John Paul II; the birth and flowering of "liberation theology" in the developing world; continuing struggles over the ordination of women and reproductive rights. There have been changes in the liturgy as well, including saying Mass in local languages; there has also been a concomitant, Latin-preserving backlash against that change. I've seen, at Glide Memorial Church, located in San Francisco's gritty Tenderloin district, contemporary social activism melded with old-fashioned, say-amen-somebody, rhythm'n'gospel worship. I've heard, in a Spanish cathedral in Peru, the Mass said in Quechua, the ancient Incan tongue. Yet I never thought that liturgical change was very important, until I attended the Planetary Mass.

When I arrived home after the Mass that night, well past midnight, it occurred to me that this was something different. The Planetary Mass is a reformulation of traditional Christian worship, and more: it is the Mass reborn for a new millennium—looking not only back, to the life of Jesus, or ahead, to eternity, but also around, to the state of the world we have inherited, and within, to the beings we can become.

Had there been a Planetary Mass in my parish twenty-five years ago, I realized, I might never have left the church.

Attending the Planetary Mass was a bona fide spiritual thrill, but would ultimately have proven frustrating if there were no hope of attending another in my area. Happily, plans are under way, according to Cliff Atkinson, editor of *Creation Spirituality* magazine, to establish a "ritual center" that will offer a range of "creation spirituality"–based programs, at the core of which will be a regular celebration of the Planetary Mass. Atkinson adds that the new center will be affiliated with the Episcopal diocese, and will be launched with the help of a small team of artists from the Nine O'Clock Service community, who will return to the San Francisco Bay area to help set up the Mass and train local people to produce it.

This, to me, is very exciting news, because the Planetary Mass is the most intriguing and promising liturgical innovation I've encountered in my own spiritual odyssey. It combines a progressive brand of Christianity with a focused sense of social justice and a fervent eco-activism; it aims at achieving a kind of psycho-social healing that our culture desperately needs; it revels in the wisdom of the body, as yet another manifestation of the glory of Creation; and, not incidentally, its aesthetic is pervasively contemporary, offering the hope of appealing strongly to young people, including my own too-hip children. And yet, all this was done in the context of a Christian canon—a rejuvenated canon, to be sure, but full of all the essential elements of a Christian service: offertory, supplication, confession, communion, fellowship.

At a time when, on the one hand, mainline churches are suffering from a continued dwindling in their memberships, and on the other hand, Christian sects such as the Pentecostals and Charismatics are enjoying record growth, worship trends are clearly at a turning point. They are also at a crossroad. People clearly want a more powerful spiritual experience, a feeling of spiritual renewal; that's why the Pentecostals and Charismatics, whose services offer reverberant, mystical experiences, attract new followers in great numbers. At the same time, there is a movement to simplify worship and faith in the same way the Disney entertainment empire remakes old fairy tales and literary classics in its own, plain-vanilla image. The Willow Creek Community Church, outside Chicago, attracts 15,000 people weekly—according to ABC-TV, it's "the best-attended church in America"—by making its services more like a night at the theater than a day in church, and by refashioning the language of its services to appeal to mass audiences. "I appreciate

that they're making it easy for me," said one parishioner. "I like things that are easy. It's like going to a
movie, only better."

However, while such efforts are clearly succeeding,
they risk losing something essential in the process.
Spirituality is not necessarily easy. What I liked about
the Planetary Mass was precisely its complexity, its in-
tricacy, its richness of detail and eclectic use of a variety of sources. What I hope to foster in my children
is not a fawning worshipfulness or a simple-minded
faith, but a pursuit of their own spiritual destinies informed by all the intelligence with which they are en-
dowed, using their critical faculties to assess their
beliefs at every step along the way. I also hope they
will bring their great depth of feeling to bear on their
spiritual search, so the world will benefit from their
open hearts and savor their compassion. And I hope
they will live to see a time when people transcend all
the fear and loathing of the physical self that has seen
us vacillate between self-abnegation and purposeless
hedonism, and finally reinhabit their bodies as instru-
ments of worship.

I see precious few of these aspects of spirituality
portended in mainstream religions, but I see a wide-
spread yearning for them abroad in the culture, and
I see them all gestating in the Planetary Mass. With
any luck, by the time you read these words, I will have

had the opportunity to bring my family to a celebration of this "postmodern" worship service, and in so doing, introduce them to a ritual sure to become a more common feature of the spiritual landscape in the decades to come.

CHAPTER 9
Toward a 21st-Century Spirituality

*O love that fires the sun
keep me burning.*
—Bruce Cockburn,
"Lord of the Starfields"

Just as our lifestyle eclipsed that of our parents and grandparents, the world our children inhabit will seem light years beyond anything we've experienced or imagined. But there is one contemporary twist to the progress of our culture as we watch the succession of generations continue: in some ways, where our lives were substantially easier than those of our parents, our children's lives will be *harder*. The world, as we perceive it in the West, anyway (through global telecommunications and the particular view they present), seems daily to grow harsher, more self-serving. The old verities of the workplace are fading; career trends change almost before the ink is dry on the latest pronouncements; meanwhile, the cost of living keeps going up while, for many, earning power keeps going down. Moreover, the peoples of the industrialized world seem to grow more and more alienated from each other and from the elements of local culture that have traditionally nurtured individual and community vitality. At the same time, the discrepancy between our standard of living and that of underdeveloped nations does not appear to be lessening. And of course, the state of regional and global ecosystems remains fragile, despite significant progress made in recent decades. So there are local, national, and global tensions that make the world, even as it becomes a more intimate place, seem a more tenuous and less hospitable one.

Our children know this. They know about polluted air and rivers; they know about absconded and abused children; they know about drug-related murders and fratricidal wars. We may try to hide it from them, we may even limit their exposure to the news media which report all this hourly, but they know about it anyway. They sense our fear for their safety and internalize it. They see grisly images in the newspapers and on TV and struggle to comprehend them. They lost their innocence long before we were ready for them to become world-weary. In the midst of these pervasive assaults on their tender sensibilities, what kind of spiritual sustenance can we give them?

We adults have our own struggle with the state of the world, and our own search for the spiritual sustenance we need to continue that struggle. But when we consider the world our children will inherit, the kind of philosophical and spiritual framework a responsible adult will need to have in order to face the day and to have a hope of living in a peaceable society becomes clearer. A "21st-Century Spirituality," if you will, would, then, include the following elements—which we must teach our children *now*:

Tolerance. I put this first on my list because it strikes me as the most vital thing in a contemporary person's spiritual toolkit. It's more tragic than ironic that it should have to be pointed out in this day and age, but trends and events of recent years indicate that we are somehow forgetting this basic element of civilized discourse.

Whatever your particular faith, however diligently you instruct your children in it, however certain you are of the absolute truth of your religion's doctrines, remember to teach your children that other cultures, and other people in your culture, subscribe to religious philosophies that differ from yours. To the extent that you may consider those philosophies erroneous, delineate *how*; to the extent that you find anything of value in their teachings, be sure to say so. (This, incidentally, can be a profound teaching exercise, for both parent and child.) But remember to point out that those philosophies were arrived at sincerely, and their adherents have the perfect right to hold their views. If we are to have any hope of seeing, or having our children see, a peaceable world, we *must* learn not to patronize other denominations or religions, or dismiss their adherents as "sinners" or "heathens."

Freedom. This may seem gratuitous in a country that "invented" religious freedom, but I mean it in two ways. First, no principle can be more important to convey to our children than that of religious freedom, i.e., that we as a people accept it as axiomatic that each individual has the absolute right to worship—or not—as he or she sees fit, free from coercion; to affiliate with a congregation or identify with a faith or pursue a highly individualized brand of spirituality, as defined only by the trajectory of that individual's soul, unfettered by anyone else's agenda, provided only that one's search does no harm to another.

But there is a second, more subtle way in which we

as parents must teach our children this indispensable lesson, and that has to do with the surprising realization that *religious freedom begins at home.* Now, you and I both know that parenting is not a democratic institution, and I am not proposing that devout parents act as if they don't care if their young charges evince a strong interest in, say, ritual cannibalism. But I do mean that there is a difference between *teaching* what you believe and *forcing* unwilling young minds to believe what they cannot accept or do not understand. Attempting the latter is a ticket to failure, while adopting the former method is not only more loving, it is more likely to put across the beliefs you wish to foster.

Moreover, children should be encouraged to express their questions, misgivings, doubts, and especially their differences of opinion or belief, for several reasons: 1) it teaches them that their opinions and beliefs matter; 2) it shows that the road to faith is not traveled blindly or without cherishing the landscape along the way; 3) throughout the history of religious philosophy, learned, revered teachers, even in the same tradition, have disagreed and dialogued endlessly, thereby deepening and furthering every student's appreciation of the insights passed on over time—and our children deserve no less; and 4) *force-fed dogma does not engender faith; it produces desper-*

ation. What we should be aiming to do is not replicating ourselves, or, in this case, our beliefs in our children, but helping them open to the process of revealing their souls' true nature to themselves. Plug them in and watch them glow, without worrying too much about the wattage or the color of the light.

Immunity from Fundamentalism. It may well be that fundamentalism (of whatever variety—Christian, Islamic, or any other kind you've got), and not commercialism, or conspicuous consumption, or excessive sexual stimulation, or drug abuse, or [Your Pet Peeve Goes Here], is the Great Societal Ill of our time. In saying this, I am in no way demeaning anyone's fervently-held beliefs, nor their right to hold them. I am, rather, considering how the rise of modern fundamentalism threatens to constrain democratic processes and deny basic, presumably inalienable, liberties, not only to believers, but most especially to nonbelievers. Where a community or nation inclines toward a fundamentalist ethos, its culture narrows, and its citizens palpably lose options in terms of mobility, well-being, livelihood, worship, even thought. If you don't believe me, ask Algerian officials trying to maintain a secular government in the face of agitation and terrorism (including assassination) by Islamic fundamentalists; or Japanese officials trying to solve the riddle of a cult (calling itself "Supreme Truth") which thinks nothing of attacking thousands on crowded subways. It's worth noting that such acts of terrorism and hatred are carried out by true believers, never by sect leaders themselves; that is, fundamentalism as a modern social phenomenon is nothing if not *manipulative*. It is less about faith than about control.

What attracts people—decent, sincere, hard-working, people, who love their children and want only a better life—to fundamentalist creeds? I believe it is the increasingly desperate state of their spirit. Life today is hard, and getting harder. Raising a family, just providing food and shelter, is difficult; few families can do it without two incomes. Technology and mass media bewilder many of us. Everywhere we turn there are new perils to our health and the well-being of our children. Old mores, and the "absolute" truths that spawned them, have dissipated. (As Bob Dylan once sang, "I got nothin', Ma, to believe in.") We can now create life under artificial conditions, and choose to avert it. Old proscriptions about sex and other pleasures of the flesh have fallen away, despite the increased risks associated with indulging in them. In the face of all this, just shouldering responsibility for one's actions and moral choices is, to many, overwhelming.

Just tell me what to do, those attracted to fundamentalism seem to be saying. *I can't handle it anymore. Tell me what's wrong and what's right. Assure me there's a better place than this, and tell me exactly what I have to do to get there. I need to believe in something unquestioningly. I need to know there is something bigger, something better, and that I can be a part of it, surrender to it. Tell me what my role is. I don't care what it is or how hard I have to work or how long it takes. Just tell me I don't have to figure it out by myself, and I won't complain.*

What does this have to do with parenting? Well, for one thing, it is absolutely the wrong message to be sending our children: we need to find ways to teach them self-reliance and resourcefulness, not helplessness and surrender of their autonomy—and we need to do this without denying or minimizing the fact that the world can be a difficult, perplexing place. For another, those of us concerned with our children's spiritual lives should encourage them to understand that the spiritual search, the journey of the soul, does not end with the first answer to the first question, or even the hundredth answer to the hundredth question. No matter how devoutly one believes in the teachings of one's faith, no matter how tidily one's cosmology explains one's world, the experience of being alive inevitably prompts questions, doubts, changes in beliefs; and there's no reason why it shouldn't. Trying to forestall questions or prohibit doubts or limit discussion or dismiss interpretation, when those are precisely the key factors in the progression of human understanding and faith—and, yes, religious doctrine—is as unnatural as trying to get a river to flow uphill.

Inquisitiveness. Along those lines, it is imperative that we encourage our children to question that which is perplexing or difficult, or just plain strikes them as wrong. They should always feel free to seek clarification of any teaching they do not fully understand, and more: they should never be "forced" to believe something they cannot in good conscience accept. I remember when the nuns at St. Aloysius taught us about "supernatural mysteries" such as The Holy Trinity. We were told that we weren't expected to *understand* it; in fact, we were told, our finite minds weren't *capable* of understanding it. Just the same, we were expected to *believe* it, to profess it. Some part of me is still angry over that, all these years later. Compelling children to believe something their innate faculties cannot decipher is teaching them to disavow the very gifts bestowed upon them to ensure their survival and success.

It is nonetheless true that parents may, through long and difficult processes of study, contemplation, conversion, and/or sincere devotion, adhere to beliefs that, simply put, require a leap of faith. They may further wish to cultivate those beliefs in their children. In such cases, parents should look to their own hearts and make their best efforts to explain their beliefs, how they arrived at them, and especially *why they hold them,* as a means of putting their experiences across to their children, and in so doing making the experiences "available" for inspection, evaluation, and adoption.

If you find yourself in this situation, ask yourself: What did I used to believe? How and when did my belief change? What were the most important influences on me? What do I remember about the places I was in, the people I heard and spoke with, the feelings I had? All those details are important to pass along to your child, and will make the story of your experience more real and engaging. And then, once you've related your experience—your journey—ask your child: Have you ever thought about this? How do *you* think it works? What have you heard other people say about it? Can you tell me a story that shows this the way you understand it? If you can engage in this process with your child, she or he may still not accept your beliefs immediately and without exception, but one thing is for sure: you will be enjoying the deepest, most rewarding communication with your beloved that you could ever hope to have. Which should be reason enough to do it. After all, the odds are pretty good that you are spending your entire life arriving at, testing, professing your beliefs, so it makes good sense to allow your kids at least that much time. In the meantime, enjoy the dialogues—and be prepared to learn a thing or two from your kids, while you're at it.

But in any case, strive to cultivate in your child a basic comfort with the act and process of questioning—dogma, gratuitous "mysteries," faceless authority. (Everything except your demand that they do their homework or clean up their room, *now*.) If more people reached adulthood with this basic instinct well-exercised, we might see fewer people surrendering their thought processes to secretive, even dangerous cults. (We'd also be less susceptible to advertising and other mass-media machinations, but that's another discussion.)

Study. Ignorance is no friend of the spirit, and a lack of information does not make one's faith stronger. We owe it to our children and ourselves not only to deepen our knowledge about our own faith, but also to learn something meaningful about other faiths—even if they hold no particular spiritual attraction for us. Those who have not yet done so will be surprised at how edifying it can be, and especially at how much they may incorporate into their own beliefs, without in any way "betraying" their faith. (Many years ago, I attended a human-potential–type seminar, at which it was announced that a high Buddhist lama would soon be coming to town. When the seminar attendees were invited to a public ceremony to be led by this lama, one woman asked, "How will this affect you if you're a Christian?" Without missing a beat, the seminar leader replied, "It'll make you a *better* one.")

I have heard too many people dismiss the scriptures of other peoples' religions as misguided, erroneous, or even diabolical, to think that what I'm suggesting will be easy for everyone. But I know that nothing I have ever read in the *Bhagavad Gita,* for instance, has ever lessened my appreciation for the Bible, nor has any visit I've ever paid to a Hindu ashram or a Buddhist temple taken away anything I ever learned from the Gospel. Quite the opposite is true: the wisdom of every faith tradition I've encountered has informed and even reinforced the beliefs I hold dear.

Some people regard other religions and their leaders as weird at best, and dangerous, even poisonous, at worst. Once, years ago, as I related some incident or aphorism having to do with a Buddhist teacher, my own mother sat in stony silence until I was done and then said somberly, "You know, we *have* a religion . . . it's the *Catholic* religion," as if to ward off any evil or otherwise unwelcome influence my anecdote might bring into her home. Today, happily, she is more comfortable with the idea that her children might be curious about other faiths, but the woman who made that comment would have been surprised to hear the Dalai Lama, the worldwide leader of Tibetan Buddhists, say, as he did when he visited San Francisco in 1994: "The West is traditionally Christian and will remain and should remain Christian. I am even skeptical of [Western] parents who are Buddhist [converts] and decide to raise their children as Buddhists. Perhaps they should let the children look at many traditions and then decide."

For that matter, Pope John Paul II, to name just one Christian leader, would benefit from increased study of Buddhism and familiarity with the Dalai Lama's words, judging the controversy provoked by his comments about it in his best-selling book *Crossing the Threshold of Hope*. Saying that Buddhism was "atheistic" and had "an almost exclusively *negative soteriology*" [emphasis in the original], (the latter word meaning "doctrine of salvation"); the Pope had written that "The 'enlightenment' experienced by Buddha comes down to the conviction that the world is bad, that it is the source of evil. . . . To *save oneself* means, above all, to free oneself from evil by becoming *indifferent to the world, which is the source of evil* [all italics in original]." Buddhist leaders were quick to point out the errors in this interpretation of their religion. The Pope hadn't "done his homework," said Reverend Ken Tanaka of the Institute for Buddhist Studies in Berkeley. "Essentially, Buddhism is about becoming detached from greed, hatred, and ignorance—not from the world."

In today's world, we are in close contact with peoples from other nations, who speak languages, wear styles of clothing, and observe customs profoundly different from our own. We accept this as a by-product of the "shrinking" of the world brought about by advances in telecommunications and transportation technology. In fact, many people relish the contact with cultures that would have remained inaccessible to them in earlier times. So it is with religion. Especially in the West, you can find out about different religions, even observe services celebrated or hear lectures delivered by high-ranking teachers or clergy. Any medium-sized bookstore or library will have an ample collection of books, including many aimed at children; most towns will have a broad sampling of the houses of worship of different denominations. Use these resources to provide your children—and yourself—with an ongoing education in the teachings and practices of other faiths, and even to see how other parishes or congregations in your own faith may differ from your own.

Consult original sources; better still, consult multiple editions, different translations. Do this for the texts of your own faith, as well as those of other religions. When you heed the teachings of your local clergy, do not let your search for understanding end there. Join a discussion or study group in your congregation; if there isn't one, start one. Share what you learn—and what you're still puzzling over—with your children, in effect starting an at-home "discussion group."

Remember that, in religion no less than in math, history, literature, science, or any other discipline, it is not possible to study, explore, or reflect too much.

Reverence for and Intimacy with Nature. Perhaps nowhere are the pitfalls of technological cultures more apparent than in our alienation from the natural world. Today, people all over the industrialized and developing world alike are working to achieve a healthier relationship with nature, ever more aware that the planet's survival—and our own—depends on it. It's no small irony that many earlier cultures had what we are working so hard to regain: a pervasive intimacy with nature, which often made life much more difficult than we would find tolerable, but also made real and immutable one's place in the infinite web of living things. I don't suggest that we try to live without electricity, telecommunications, pharmaceuticals, or modern shelter, but clearly we have a long way to go to restore the balance between humans and the planet that has sustained them for thousands of generations. It is incumbent upon us to foster in our children a sensibility that will commit them intellectually to, and connect them spiritually with, their Mother, the Earth.

The good news for parents is that children come predisposed to this sensibility; they are keenly receptive to the processes and incremental miracles of nature. My own son Gabe, for instance, at the age of five or six, was a typically high-octane youngster: a grand-slam-hitting, Ninja-Turtle-emulating, big-sister-fighting, explosive bundle of boy. But with a spade or a garden hose in his hand, he became a reflective, doe-eyed devotee of photosynthesis. He would pick peas from our backyard garden with a zen-like mindfulness and serenity that seemed missing from his other endeavors. And, like his brother and sister (and your kids too, I suspect), he had, and still has, an almost preternatural affinity with other creatures and their life cycles. One day we came home to find that his pet rabbit had inexplicably died; when we summoned up the courage to tell him, he calmly said, as if to reassure *us,* "That's okay. He'll come back to life in another form."

Even parents who might find it difficult or awkward to adopt a formal spiritual practice or join a particular congregation can find great spiritual riches and boundless joy by exploring the mystical experience of the natural world. It's not hard to do; in fact, it's hard to go wrong. Almost no matter what your living situation, you can integrate animals and plants into it. Our own very urban household has, over the years, been inhabited by one dog, six cats, one rabbit, several goldfish, one snake, three parakeets, and, currently, one iguana and two "flame-belly toads." My kids have also had intimate encounters with houseplants and home-grown fruits and vegetables (many of which they planted and tended themselves), even in our postage-stamp-sized yard. Some of the earliest meal blessings they ever heard focused on the splendid good fortune of living in a world that naturally produced fuel for our bodies. They didn't have to be told twice.

The point is not that my wife and I are paragons of naturalist homemaking—we're not—but that if we can do it, so can you. And there is much more all of us can do, if we just use our imaginations. Encourage your children to know the names, textures, colors, smells, and, where appropriate, tastes, of as many local and regional species as possible. Let them see your own wonder, delight, surprise; hug a tree or jump in a lake or caress an ear of corn, and urge them to do the same. Create a backyard "wildlife sanctuary" of a size and scale appropriate to your situation, even if all you can do is put up a hummingbird feeder. Spend time with your kids just listening to the music of the wind in the trees; the birds conversing; lying on a hillside finding pictures in the clouds; and digging up a square foot of soil to count the different bugs that are happily composting it.

Whether or not you believe in a Creator, it is always possible to experience the blessings of "creation." And if you can encourage your children to see themselves as members of the family of living things, as magical beings whose own bodies grow and heal and learn and long to live just as the flowers and trees and furry critters around them do, you will bequeath them a gift as precious as the life you gave them—one that will serve them the rest of their days.

Honor for the Feminine. Even after twenty or more years of feminist advances, there is still a strong sentiment abroad to subjugate women, ranging from the exhortations of the "Promise Keepers," a latter-day

Christian men's movement, that husbands should "lead" their wives, to the vestigial barbarism of ritual clitoridectomies in some developing countries. How could we have gone so wrong? What could men possibly be so afraid of in women? Why is it so difficult for men, even today, to learn to accept women as equal partners, as fellow travelers, as cocreators of our destiny?

Those questions are outside the scope of this book, and I do not have tidy answers to them. But I do know that it is our responsibility as parents in the waning years of this century to instill in our children some other way of regarding themselves and the opposite gender—a way that will enhance their appreciation of both while taking away nothing from either. This affects their spiritual lives as well as their social, political, and economic lives; in fact, it could be said that the kind of appreciation they will need in their lifetimes can only be learned through their spirituality.

On this score, our children are fortunate in one respect, at least: they are living in a time when women are preaching and being ordained in many denominations, testifying to their faiths with fervor and erudition at least equal to that of their male counterparts. If you are choosing among various congregations, and one sponsors female clergy where others do not, all else being equal, consider choosing the more egalitarian congregation for the important lesson that it will teach your children (and indeed, your whole family).

But there is so much more that each individual and family can do to nurture reverence for the Feminine in our world. Begin with the females in your family. I was taught by my father to honor my mother above everyone else, even though he was to be considered the final "authority" (although truth to tell, my parents had, and have, a more equal partnership than did many of their peers); and I have tried to build on that. It requires continual effort on my part to understand what it means to be a man in today's world, to endeavor to be that kind of man, and to cherish the many women in my life and the world at large. I am not always successful, thanks to my own shortcomings or the deleterious impact of the culture around us. But I keep trying, because I want it that way, because my life is more satisfying to the extent I succeed, and because I owe nothing less to my sons, daughter, and wife.

The most natural place to begin, it seems to me, is with the fundamental fact of biology: a mother literally surrenders her body to the act of bearing a child, enduring great pain and risking her own well-being to bring her beloved to life. This simple truth contains the wildness of nature, the fragility of existence, the exquisite design of reproductive biology, the frightening power of love, and the ineffability of the Great Mystery all in one observable event. I remember getting hints of that truth with the births of my younger siblings, and I have tried to bring my children more closely into contact with it. We never stop learning about that truth, either; I picked up a bit more of it recently, when I sent my mom a Mother's Day card that said simply, "God's greatest gift is a mother's heart."

Children taught to cherish the great sacrifice their mothers made for them—note that I don't mean they should feel *guilty* for it, but rather *thankful*—will already be on their way to honoring women. But boys and girls, men and women, fathers and mothers, can find ways to reinforce that every day. In terms of their spirituality, we should take care, as parents, not to hold female religious teachers in lesser esteem than males, simply on the basis of their gender. We should seek out and familiarize ourselves and our children with stories of female saints and holy persons, along with men whose lives inspire us. We can study the mythologies and practices of matristic cultures—those whose worldviews were formed in a time "when God was a woman"—and teach our children that God was not (and is not) always seen as an omnipotent male with a long, flowing beard.

We live in an age of backlash; recently, a novelist friend of mine was accused by a columnist for a major metropolitan daily newspaper of having provoked the ire of the nation's "angry white males" because she authored a successful (and delightful) account of a Goddess-oriented culture in Neolithic Europe. Those same angry men are given credit for the Republican victories in the 1994 midterm elections, and the excesses of "feminazis" are said to be responsible for the anti-affirmative-action fervor seemingly sweeping the nation as I write. Perhaps if these "victims" of equal opportunity had been taught that it lessens their manhood not one whit to honor, celebrate, and respect the females of the species—indeed, to recognize and appreciate the introspective, receptive, "yin," i.e., feminine, side of their own nature—they would be less agitated, and men and women would be less at odds with each other. Then, perhaps, we could pursue our own growth and support each other's advancement with great mutual satisfaction; we might even be able to *get along*. Imagine that! If this vision is appealing to you, teach your sons and daughters to accept equally the blessings of maleness and femaleness, in the material world *and* the world of the spirit.

Respect for Indigenous Traditions. In a sense, the previous two elements come together here, for indigenous peoples have in many instances maintained a more pervasive and intimate awareness of nature, and sustained a deeper appreciation for women, in the form of councils, matrilineal heritage, and deference to elders, especially matriarchs. But there is a broader sense in which I believe we must cultivate our own and our children's knowledge of and respect for native cultures and their spiritual traditions.

Throughout the history of Christendom, certainly, the propagation of the faith has meant the conversion of indigenous populations, at times by forceful means. European Christians had no monopoly on this; all over the world peoples have overrun each other, and indigenous tribes have not hesitated to conquer and subjugate their neighbors when they felt it suited their purposes. But today, with the Judeo-Christian ethos dominating in the West, and native traditions in eclipse, something vital to the human experience is on the brink of extinction.

Psychologist Chellis Glendinning calls it the "primal matrix." I think of her term as the place where biology, psychology, and spirituality intersect: a level of awareness so fundamentally integrated with the natural phenomena of one's own body and the surrounding ecosphere that there is essentially no separation between the individual and the world at large. When a Hopi farmer stands on his windswept mesa and calls for rain so that the sacred corn can grow, he is articulating his faith, to be sure, but he is also working within a system whose operating principles he knows well.

I don't know if we can recapture that integrated consciousness, or incorporate it into our modern culture. But I do know that as indigenous cultures expire, their tragedy—the loss of their way of life—is also *our* tragedy: the loss of a vast archive of knowledge and experience as natural beings. Now, there's natural and then there's *natural,* you might say: it's entirely possible to be a "natural being" even in a densely urban environment. I don't mean to fall prey to the modern impulse to romanticize native peoples or demonize ourselves. It is nonetheless true that we live in a time where the survival of numerous indigenous peoples is in doubt, and our children's world will be vastly poorer if we do not make a concerted effort to help those peoples and their cultures survive.

Recent years have seen greatly accelerated interest in native spirituality, especially in North America—to the point where many tribal leaders castigate New Age authors and teachers for expropriating ancient traditions, and white middle-class seekers for being "Indian wannabes." Clearly this trend has at least in part degenerated into a fad that amounts to nothing more than a latter-day game of "Cowboys and Indians," with the good guys' and bad guys' roles reversed. But just because some people might be exploitive, and others gullible, doesn't mean that those who are sincerely trying to undo the damage heaped upon their Western-bred souls shouldn't look to Native American wisdom to inform their effort. And what I am proposing is not that we raise our children to be pretend Indians, but that we teach them more about those who inhabited the land than we learned at their age. And that we incorporate what we learn into our own spiritual voices.

Today there are wonderful resources available to familiarize ourselves and our children with Native American history and culture—books and other publications, museums and other institutions, audio-visual materials, and so on. I have especially enjoyed reading my children the stories Joseph Bruchac has collected and written. I am always struck by the way in which these stories show us how ancient peoples saw other creatures as "people"—rabbit people, deer people, bird people—and themselves as just another kind of creature. For that matter, the sky, sun, moon, stars, rivers, and wind—all were seen as organisms, with powers and domains that humans had to recognize and heed. How much more vital a spiritual life would you and I lead if we similarly construed our every act, every interaction, every minute of the day, as an encounter with other spirits, another in the ceaseless progression of living things? It's not for nothing that theologian Matthew Fox takes so much of the inspiration for his "creation spirituality" from native traditions.

So, read these stories, especially "creation stories," to your children. Most families can also find opportunities for exposure to Native American history and culture unique to their locale and situation—state and national parks, national monuments, reservations, and other sites permitting visits—and those may provide the most powerful way to cultivate an appreciation of indigenous traditions. Discuss with your children the ways in which your spiritual practices both differ from and parallel theirs.

Skepticism. Reason and faith are not enemies; they just don't serve the same purpose. I once heard Bucky Fuller, when asked by *New Dimensions* host Michael Toms what he "believed" about something or other, say, "I don't believe *anything*, old man." His point was that he only held to ideas that made sense to him given what he could prove empirically. Yet this same resolutely scientific thinker was convinced that the Universe was "designed." You and I might say that the very notion of a Designer is an article of faith; for Bucky it followed logically from observable phenomena. Either way, I see Bucky's remark, and his other descriptions of the Universe's architecture, as a clear statement on the proper relationship between reason and faith. And our children will certainly need to know about *that* in the next century.

When I say that we should cultivate skepticism in our children, I don't mean we should train them never to believe in anything. The world is full of intelligent, educated people who refuse to believe something that doesn't fit their notion of what is possible, even if evidence suggests otherwise; we don't need more of those. But we do need more people—and our children will need to be the kind of people—who are open to suggestions and new ideas and comfortable with entertaining other perspectives, yet who are not easily swayed. We need people who will not surrender their will or go against their own good judgment just because some charismatic figure—entertainer, politician, or religious leader—says so, and people who will not be overly susceptible to exploitation and manipulation, whether by infomercials or televangelists.

In order to develop a healthy skepticism, or, to put

it more neutrally, critical thinking in our children, we need to foster "media literacy" in them, so they can sift through the endless barrage of messages the mass media direct at them daily. We also need to encourage them to think deeply and carefully about the ideas and doctrines we are asking them to embrace. No doctrine that cannot withstand such scrutiny is worthy of them; and any teaching that does hold up under thorough analysis is likely to serve them well through all their days.

Ease with Uncertainty. Who knows? Who *really* knows? Do you? Does your preacher? Do the great sages of the ages? Do the Scriptures? Do professors of religion? Does the Pope, the Dalai Lama, the highest mullah or holiest swami? Have they been to the other side and come back to show us incontrovertible proof? How do we know whom God speaks through and who is a sincere fool (or, worse, a charlatan)? Who among us has not harbored grave doubts, found some questions unanswerable, struggled to know only to remain perplexed or at least unsure?

Uncertainty is the crucible of faith: when we cannot know, what we believe is what offers us comfort, provides us hope, takes us in the direction we feel we should go. Sometimes faith produces a kind of transcendent knowing born of the very act of believing. But too many of us make the error of then thinking that uncertainty has no place in the believer's heart, let alone the seeker's quest. The gravest manifestation of this error can be seen in the fundamentalist mind-set. As Ira Rifkin, assistant editor of the *Baltimore Jewish Times* and a longtime observer of fundamentalism in its various forms, has written, fundamentalists "are connected to the rest of us by their spiritual struggle with doubt and fear—the same doubt and fear that I, for one, continually wrestle with as well. Where they differ from me is in their response to this struggle. They have chosen to demonize doubt itself. Church doctrine or Biblical text becomes the universal answer to difficult contemporary issues." Rifkin adds that "one does not have to be a card-carrying member of the religious right to exhibit symptoms" of this mind-set: "Ever talk to people who with disturbing certainty insist that *their* guru, *their* diet, or *their* spiritual view is the only one that makes sense—regardless of any evidence to the contrary?" The irony of this mind-set is that it ultimately impoverishes the true believer's spiritual search, for spiritual knowledge is like other forms of knowing: it is revealed in layers, as one's understanding becomes more sophisticated, one's questions more focused, one's experience deeper and detours more numerous—and one becomes more familiar, more comfortable, with uncertainty and doubt.

Children require the security that comes with knowing beyond a doubt that they are loved and cared for; likewise, they do not take easily, when young, to epistemological uncertainties, notwithstanding their natural inquisitiveness. They want you to know already what they don't know yet. But where you don't know something, you will do them no great service by pretending you do. (Besides which, if you make something up on the spot, they will sniff it out!)

So, by all means, teach your children what you know and believe. Just don't forget to point out where you're not sure, what you wonder about, and even— especially—what you question. Show them that you can actually be fascinated by a Big Question and reasonably comfortable with not having a steel-trap answer to it. (Remember: if you do nothing more than introduce them to the Mystery, you'll have done plenty!) If you can, talk about how really working with a particular question or doubt of yours resulted in a deeper understanding of the world or appreciation of being alive. After you've done your best to explain your beliefs and the limits of your knowledge, ask them what *they* think, how they see it. Even if their answers shock or dismay you, be patient. Listen.

Could their ideas offer you some new way of looking at your own beliefs, point toward some new understanding? In any case, this is likely not the last chance you'll have to discuss these matters with your children. In the meantime, you will have shown them that doubts and questions are not bad habits to be avoided, but important tools given to us in order to help us find our way.

Responsibility. In the Judeo-Christian tradition, we have guilt, sin, and punishment; in Eastern religions these concepts appear as the more helpful construct of *karma*. I am oversimplifying only a little: in the West, when we think of responsibility, we are as likely as not to be thinking of atonement and obligation and punitive damages as we are of the individual's rightful actions in a given situation. Whereas the concept of *karma* teaches that one's actions in the world attach to one's spiritual destiny. In other words, in the West we tend to think of the universe—that is, God—as being fundamentally concerned with how "good" or "bad" an individual is, as measured by her or his actions; but anyone familiar with Hinduism or Buddhism understands that the universe doesn't *care* whether one is "good" or "bad," being content to let the law of *karma* equalize right and wrong actions over the course of eternity. In more practical terms,

Western societies, having attended to legal definitions of what is "right" and "responsible," seem to turn on what individuals, communities, and corporations can *get away with*—clearly a perversion of the idea of "responsibility"—while a student of *karma* knows that *no one "gets away with" anything*. Thus, a "responsible" corporation can commit egregious acts of pollution and still be a "good" citizen. In the East, no one would want that corporation's *karma*, no matter how lucrative its business.

Our newfound enthusiasm for "responsibility" as a vital part of the social contract is doomed to failure unless we revisit what we mean by it. Moreover, our children will never become responsible unless we teach them that the word means something more than "the minimal amount you have to do to get the rest of the world off your case." In order to grow into financially, socially, and spiritually responsible adults, children need to learn that responsibility means, simply, *owning your actions*. It means telling the truth, cleaning up your mess, facing what's in front of you, being unafraid. It means avoiding harm to others, even when that would be "permitted," for it means understanding that, according to *karma*, or "the law of return," you get what you give in this world— "what goes around comes around." Most of all, it means making choices in every situation based on an awareness of the full impact of your choices—for good or for ill—in the world around you.

The first and foremost way to teach this to our children, of course, is to model it ourselves. (Hey, I never said this would be *easy!*) Letting your children see you "owning" an awkward or difficult consequence of your actions will go a lot farther than endless exhortations on the subject. Recently I had an unexpected opportunity to do just this. One afternoon Gabe and Jessamine were sitting around the kitchen table, kibitzing boisterously, having a good time. Gabe accidentally knocked over a blackberry smoothie Jessamine had just made for herself. The drink spilled into her lap, threatening to ruin her new slacks. Gabe was faced with the prospect of having to buy his sister a new pair of slacks. I should point out that Gabe was not keen on the idea of spending a fair chunk of his savings in this manner.

Moreover, he felt that, since he had not *intended* to spill the drink, he shouldn't be held "responsible." (It seems the legalistic interpretation of the word extends even to preteens.) I gently explained to him that, although I was sure he hadn't *meant* to spill the drink, he nonetheless had *done* it, and that it was up to him to make the situation right. This only made him more frustrated; he felt his innocence of intent should count for something. And it did. "No one's mad at you," I explained. "I can tell you're sorry about it." But I didn't really get the point across until I told him about something I'd done just a day or two earlier.

I had borrowed a rented video from our neighbor Alan and promised to return it in time to avoid any additional charges. I personally dropped the video off right on time—at the wrong store. When Alan wound up having to pay for an extra night, and we figured out what happened, I reimbursed him without complaint or hesitation. "See," I told Gabe, "I not only didn't mean for it to be late, I made *sure* it wasn't late. But I made a mistake. And I paid for my mistake, because it was *my* mistake, not Alan's. He wasn't mad at me, and I wasn't mad at him, or even at myself. It just happened, and I did it, and I took care of it." Hearing this calmed Gabe down a little. He calmed down a lot more when his sister's slacks came out of the wash without a trace of stain, but the point had been made. Young children have a hard time with the concept of responsibility, but by the time kids reach the age of ten or twelve they can begin to learn that their actions have consequences, and if we can focus our disciplinary lessons in that direction instead of toward guilt and retribution, they will learn far more about personal responsibility than any number of admonitions about sin and damnation will ever teach them.

Compassion. Often, when we speak of compassion, we mean something like "pity": heartfelt sadness at another's pain or misfortune. That can be a noble impulse, and can lead to great generosity of spirit and deed. But it is not the kind of compassion I am after, and am commending to you.

True compassion, we might say, is what we would feel toward humanity if we could think with the mind of God: fully aware of the intricacies and paradoxes of the world, intimately familiar with the joys and vicissitudes of life, the triumphs and struggles of living creatures, the setbacks and achievements of human beings toiling ceaselessly to survive, find happiness, grasp meaning. From this perspective we might feel a combination of admiration, benevolence, detachment, and empathy toward this species with so much promise, obstinance, resourcefulness, and denseness. Well, we may not be able to enjoy God's box seats or borrow God's ultra-high IQ, but we can know compassion for our fellow beings and for ourselves, and teach it to our children.

Every soul has a destiny. Every life has an arc. Every mind must confront these simple truths. Accepting this premise sows compassion. When you see your child first experience the shock of realizing that every living thing must die, you are feeling compassion. When you find yourself denying your own mortality, reserve a little compassion for yourself; it will help keep you purposeful and avoid inflicting gratuitous pain or useless self-loathing. (As the popular Buddhist-meditation teacher Jack Kornfield says in *Buddha's Little Instruction Book,* "If your compassion does not include yourself, it is incomplete.") When you encounter someone who is stuck in petty concerns or can't see past their own conceits, or who in your view is making a notable error or just plain *wrong,* the compassionate thing to do is to avoid the desire to judge or try to change the other person, in favor of offering them an insight or clue that may help them awaken. "What a pity that man dies before he awakes," the legendary spiritual teacher George Gurdjieff is supposed to have said; in this life, few enough of us ever awaken, or manage to *stay* awake. More commonly, we seem to take turns sleeping. Compassion begins in understanding that we all start out as sleepwalkers in this life.

Not surprisingly, we teach our children compassion by being compassionate, by heeding the Buddhist admonition, "Cold eye, warm heart"—that is, by seeing things as they are, not merely as we would like them to be, and doing so with great empathy. When your child comes to you with a worry or problem or pain, don't dismiss it with a simple, "It's not that bad" or "It'll go away," no matter how earnest. Acknowledge the hurt, trouble, or grief. Feel it as you have felt it yourself, and let your child know you *have* felt it yourself. After you have validated the child's experience, heard his or her concern and articulated it back in a way that makes clear you "get it," *then* you can gently begin to offer the healing advice and wise counsel the child came to you for. Offer it as subtly, in as understated a manner, as you can—phrase it as a question, or tell it as an anecdote rather than an admonition. Speak to the deepest part of your child, as if you could address her or his soul directly. Instead of revealing a secret treasure, provide a map, or a few clues, or a key; although it goes against most parents' instincts, it is not compassionate to short-circuit a child's spiritual process.

Equally important, let them see your compassion for others—and especially for yourself, as you carry out your own spiritual process. "I learned something important today," you might say as dinner begins. "I wish I knew that before, but at least I know it now." Or, offer a prayer together for our political leaders, who every day must make difficult decisions, many of which will cause some people difficulty, even cost some people their lives, but who must nonetheless make those decisions because the world requires it of them: pray for them to find it possible to act sincerely according to their conscience, and with compassion. Each day brings us countless opportunities to be compassionate; with an open heart and a little imagination, you shouldn't find it hard to teach your children compassion, and, incidentally, learn about it yourself.

Coda:
Roads of the Spirit

When I was a boy, and used to attend Mass regularly, one of my favorite lines from the liturgy was the closing admonition in Latin, "Ite, missa est"—"Go, you are dismissed." The comedian in me would chuckle at the thought that the priest celebrating Mass was essentially saying, "G'wan—*get outta heah!*" But upon reflection, and even years later, long after I stopped going to church regularly, that leave-taking phrase held a particular resonance for me, as a kind of triumphal coda of the worship service. Its deeper meaning was something like, "We're done here, so you can go; but take this feeling with you and nurture it." In that spirit, and without presuming to compare my work to the 2,000-year-old Mass, I'd like to offer a few closing thoughts which I hope will further your search.

Despite the fact that people do good, heroic, virtuous things every day, ours is an age of anxiety and longing, of dissipating traditions and thoughtless change, of soul-corroding ruptures in the human community. Those who achieve some grasp of eternal verities can consider themselves truly blessed; families who, like those featured in this book, have found rituals, prayers, and other viable ways to pursue their spiritual life together discover a kind of treasure others may search for their entire lives. Many people continue to struggle with questions about the existence of God, the afterlife, and how best to find a venue for expressing their hopes and fulfilling their deepest spiritual needs. Others, meanwhile, have simply given up, or at least resigned themselves to living and eventually dying, without hope of redemption or enlightenment, in an uncaring, accidental universe. Under the circumstances, it's no wonder that so many children are adrift today. How can they be expected to believe in things that have eluded their parents?

Looked at a certain way, it boils down to the problem of faith. Recently a good friend called me to invite me to lunch; by way of previewing what she wanted to talk about, she said bluntly, "I'm struggling with my faith—I'm struggling to *find* it." I knew exactly what she meant, for I've struggled with much the same thing for most of my adult life, as have many of my friends. Her words were the plaintive cry of someone with an open heart and a willing soul, but no clear, bell-ringing path to follow, no creed to live by, no sacred city on the hill toward which to trek. Spiritually speaking, we are all dressed up with nowhere to go. If we but knew the destination, or even what bus would take us there, we could be at ease, no matter how long and arduous the journey was revealed to be; but that one thing we so fervently wish to know is the one piece of information withheld from us (until, it seems, the last possible moment).

In the absence of that knowledge, we seek faith. Many people understand faith to mean belief in God, and that is surely a large part of what we mean when we use the word; but we can talk about the meaning and value of faith in more practical terms as well. Faith is the abiding belief that we *will* find out what we need to know, that we *are* on the right path. Faith is also the sense that things are as they should be, even if they don't seem like it—that things will turn out right even if they aren't going right at the moment. Thus, faith can enable us to endure hardship, privation, pain, and doubt, comforted by the knowledge that all is unfolding according to the plan of Higher Intelligence, or at least, by the belief that things can't stay this bad forever.

But what are we to do when faith eludes us? How can we believe when we reach out and grasp nothing? What are we to teach our children, when we don't know what we have learned? Some devout people may argue that God does not turn away from those who earnestly seek refuge, and I, for one, cannot argue that they are wrong. But I know too many people who have longed for the comfort of faith and not yet found it, for me to think that the quest is always as simple as that. Perhaps it is not for us to know the particulars of this process; perhaps it is just a matter of individual souls finding their own destinies. Whatever is truly at work here, it is clear that many people hunger for the clarity and resolve they hope will accrue from the faith they hope to find. And that until they do, some part of them, too, is adrift.

If you, as a parent, feel this way, here is what I encourage you to consider: *Your children are the path to your faith.*

By this I mean two things. One, that the role of parent, while it may stir up a profound spiritual dilemma (especially if you have not settled on a particular religious practice), also engages you in the very process needed to awaken you: being a parent requires you to be aware, responsible, impeccable, honest, compassionate, loving, and concerned with the Highest Possible Good—all the things that are required on the spiritual journey, but that so many of us find easy to ignore or leave undeveloped in ourselves while only (!) our own physical and spiritual well-being is at stake. Being the best possible parent you can be means being the best possible person you can be; if that's not the purpose of a spiritual practice, what is?

Secondly, when you behold your child, you are encountering the most compelling argument for having faith that anyone can conjure. Mark Twain is supposed to have said that children were proof that God wanted the world to continue; the child before you is living testament to the irresistible force of nature, of Life, of the Desire to Be that has continued unabated since the first carbon-based life forms emerged. You can live a hundred lifetimes without ever "believing in God" for a single moment, but you cannot hold a child for even a heartbeat, let alone watch one grow, without finding yourself suffused with awe, wonder, reverence, and . . . faith. Not the kind of faith that displaces all fear, perhaps (as my family has learned); not a faith that erases all doubt, if there is such a thing. Maybe not even religious faith, if that means something concrete to you like belief in God or awareness of a Plan that includes a specific role for you personally. But faith that you and your family are part of something larger, that timeless processes are at work in you and your children, that somewhere deep in you there is an innate knowledge of what to do, or the ability to find out. In short, we and our children connect each other to eternity, as did we and our parents, as will our children and our grandchildren, and so on. (For bonus points: what other ways are there to connect to eternity? Hint: having children isn't the *only* way.)

If faith is what you seek, and it seems the thing most absent from the landscape of your life, take your child's face into your hands and gaze into her eyes. Ask him to tell you a story. Invite yourself into their daydreams. And then, "Consider the lilies of the field, how they grow . . ." You, your children, and the lilies of the field—it's a pretty decent arrangement, when you stop and think about it.

If you have not yet found a spiritual path you feel is right for you and your family: keep walking.

Even if you do not yet have faith, have faith that you may yet find it; and if you can't do that, then have faith in the faith your children have in you.

* * *

Being a parent, of course, also requires a kind of vigilance that may seem incompatible with starry-eyed mysticism. And we must remember, while being our children's devotees, that it is our job to guide them, to teach, to lead by example, to represent authority and make difficult decisions and bear heavy responsibilities. But let us not forsake the one side of parenting for the other; let us try to remain open, inquisitive, receptive, even while we must be decisive, authoritative, unyielding. (If parenting is a spiritual journey, it is certainly not without its paradoxes.) And let us not delude ourselves that we are in "control"; we are in the act of raising up human beings, and talking about spiritual destiny: control's got nothing to do with it.

Which is probably as it should be. Whether your family has a well-developed spiritual practice or not, in time your children are likely to plot their own spiritual coordinates and find themselves actively involved in the pursuit of their own spiritual trajectory. During the time I was working on this book, and worrying again about how little sustenance I'd provided my children, my daughter Jessamine, at the age of sixteen, joined a youth group at a nearby Lutheran church, quite of her own volition and at the invitation of a friend; soon thereafter the group spent spring break down in Baja California doing construction work at an orphanage there. My wife and I were surprised, pleased, and perplexed all at once. What prompted this? Was our daughter becoming a missionary? Did she want to study the Bible? Where did we go wrong/right?

Jessamine was a bit curious about the Bible and intrigued by the group's discussions, but that's not what attracted her to the group. Nor was a yen for missionary work; in fact, a month or two after the trip to Baja, she stopped going to the group—not out of any dissatisfaction, it seems, but because she became involved in other things. It seems that what led her to become involved was a constitutional attraction to life-affirming activity, and, more particularly, her affinity for helping others. Which, it becomes more apparent as she plans for college (and she discovers her interest in psychology, and envisions a career in counseling), is a central focus of hers—i.e., quite possibly, her *sadhana*.

What did Michelle and I do to provoke this? Essentially, nothing. All we did is love her. Seek and hope for the best for her. "See the Buddha" in her. Would she have been better served by a more well-defined spiritual practice in our home? Quite likely. Is she capable nonetheless of finding her way? Absolutely; she's doing it already. Is it too late for us to continue searching for ways to express our family spirituality? No, it can *never* be too late to continue, or begin; it can only be too early to finish.

My family's search is not over; in some ways, after the better part of twenty years, it's just beginning. The only thing I've forsaken is the long-ago suspicion that the search would be fruitless. Indeed, I've learned that the search is the treasure. Sometimes, the closer I get to thinking I know what I want, the further away it seems to be, but the happier I am to keep going. Perhaps you and your family find yourselves in a similar situation. If so, we can walk together.

Author's Note

I'd like to hear about you and your family—how you are walking your spiritual path—and learn how *Raising Spiritual Children in a Material World* may have aided you on your way.

I'd also like to invite you to receive and fill out the "Spirituality and the Family" survey, which first appeared in *New Age Journal*, and which led to this book. Everyone who completes and returns this survey will receive a Family Spirituality Resources listing I compiled, as my way of saying, "Thanks for letting me hear from you." To receive this survey, simply write to the address below:

Raising Spiritual Children
2550 Shattuck Ave. #94
Berkeley, CA 94704

I look forward to hearing from you. Until then, many blessings on you and your family!